William Shake
Twelfth N

In Plain and Simple English

A SwipeSpeare™ Book
www.SwipeSpeare.com

© 2012. All Rights Reserved.

Table of Contents

ABOUT THIS SERIES 3

CHARACTERS 4

PLAY 5

   ACT I 6
      SCENE I. DUKE ORSINO's palace. 6
      SCENE II. The sea-coast. 9
      SCENE III. OLIVIA'S house. 13
      SCENE IV. DUKE ORSINO's palace. 22
   ACT II 45
      SCENE I. The sea-coast. 46
      SCENE II. A street. 49
      SCENE III. OLIVIA's house. 52
      SCENE IV. DUKE ORSINO's palace. 63
      SCENE V. OLIVIA's garden. 71
   ACT III 82
      SCENE I. OLIVIA's garden. 83
      SCENE II. OLIVIA's house. 93
      SCENE III. A street. 98
      SCENE IV. OLIVIA's garden. 101
   ACT IV 123
      SCENE I. Before OLIVIA's house. 124
      SCENE II. OLIVIA's house. 128
      SCENE III. OLIVIA's garden. 135
   ACT V 137
      SCENE I. Before OLIVIA's house. 138

About This Series

The "SwipeSpeare™" series started as a way of telling Shakespeare for the modern reader—being careful to preserve the themes and integrity of the original. Visit our website SwipeSpeare.com to see other books in the series, as well as the interactive, and swipe-able, app!

The series is expanding every month. Visit BookCaps.com to see non-Shakespeare books in this series, and while you are there join the Facebook page, so you are first to know when a new book comes out.

Characters

ORSINO, Duke of Illyria

SEBASTIAN, a young Gentleman, brother to Viola

ANTONIO, a Sea Captain, friend to Sebastian

A SEA CAPTAIN, friend to Viola

VALENTINE, Gentleman attending on the Duke

CURIO, Gentleman attending on the Duke

SIR TOBY BELCH, Uncle of Olivia

SIR ANDREW AGUE-CHEEK.

MALVOLIO, Steward to Olivia

FABIAN, Servant to Olivia

CLOWN, Servant to Olivia.

OLIVIA, a rich Countess

VIOLA, in love with the Duke

MARIA, Olivia's Woman.

Lords, Priests, Sailors, Officers, Musicians, and other Attendants.

Play

ACT I

SCENE I. DUKE ORSINO's palace.

Enter DUKE ORSINO, CURIO, and other Lords; Musicians attending

DUKE ORSINO
If music be the food of love, play on;
Give me excess of it, that, surfeiting,
The appetite may sicken, and so die.
That strain again! it had a dying fall:
O, it came o'er my ear like the sweet sound,
That breathes upon a bank of violets,
Stealing and giving odour! Enough; no more:
'Tis not so sweet now as it was before.
O spirit of love! how quick and fresh art thou,
That, notwithstanding thy capacity
Receiveth as the sea, nought enters there,
Of what validity and pitch soe'er,
But falls into abatement and low price,
Even in a minute: so full of shapes is fancy
That it alone is high fantastical.

If music is what feeds love, keep playing; Give me more than I need of it, which, without having enough, The desire for love might starve, and then die. That sound again! it got quieter and quieter; Oh, it came over my ear like the sweet sound, That drifts over a field of violets, Stealing and then giving away the scent! Enough; no more: It is not as sweet now as it was before. Oh the spirit of love! You are so quick and fresh, That, no matter your depth Takes in as much as the sea; nothing enters there, No matter how real and strong, That doesn't become less and cheaper, Even in a minute: affection is so full of imagination That by itself it is fantasy.

CURIO
Will you go hunt, my lord?

Will you go hunt, my lord?

DUKE ORSINO
What, Curio?

What, Curio

CURIO
The hart.

The hart [a kind of deer, but sounding like "heart"].

DUKE ORSINO
Why, so I do, the noblest that I have:
O, when mine eyes did see Olivia first,
Methought she purged the air of pestilence!
That instant was I turn'd into a hart;
And my desires, like fell and cruel hounds,
E'er since pursue me.

Why, indeed I do, the most noble that I have: Oh, when I first saw Olivia, I thought she took all the poison from the world! In that moment I was turned into a heart; And my desires, like evil and cruel hunting dogs, Have been chasing me ever since.

Enter VALENTINE

How now! what news from her?

So, what's going on? Any news from her?

VALENTINE
So please my lord, I might not be admitted;
But from her handmaid do return this answer:

My lord, I am afraid I was not allowed to see her; But her maid gave me this answer:

The element itself, till seven years' heat,
Shall not behold her face at ample view;
But, like a cloistress, she will veiled walk
And water once a day her chamber round
With eye-offending brine: all this to season
A brother's dead love, which she would keep fresh
And lasting in her sad remembrance.

DUKE ORSINO
O, she that hath a heart of that fine frame
To pay this debt of love but to a brother,
How will she love, when the rich golden shaft
Hath kill'd the flock of all affections else
That live in her; when liver, brain and heart,
These sovereign thrones, are all supplied, and fill'd
Her sweet perfections with one self king!
Away before me to sweet beds of flowers:
Love-thoughts lie rich when canopied with bowers.

The sun itself, unless after giving the heat of seven years all at once, Would not be able to easily see her face; But, like a nun, she will walk with a veil over her face And spread salt water around her room Once a day, in order to honor Her love for her dead brother, which she wants to keep fresh And lasting in her sad memories.

Oh, she has a good heart, To pay so much love and sacrifice just to a brother, How will she love, when fate and time Has killed her ability to love anything else That might be found inside her; when her liver, brain, and heart, Those ruling thrones, are all occupied and filled Her sweet virtues with one person as king! Let me go now to sweet beds of flowers: Thoughts of love are richer when covered with garden plants.

Exeunt

SCENE II. The sea-coast.

Enter VIOLA, a Captain, and Sailors

VIOLA
What country, friends, is this?

What country, friends, is this?	

Captain
This is Illyria, lady.

This is Illyria, lady.

VIOLA
And what should I do in Illyria?
My brother he is in Elysium.
Perchance he is not drown'd: what think you, sailors?

*And what should I do now that I'm in Illyria?
My brother is in Heaven.
Unless by some chance he is not drowned: what do you think, sailors?*

Captain
It is perchance that you yourself were saved.

It was by chance that you yourself were saved.

VIOLA
O my poor brother! and so perchance may he be.

Oh my poor brother! And so maybe he will be saved by luck

Captain
True, madam: and, to comfort you with chance,
Assure yourself, after our ship did split,
When you and those poor number saved with you
Hung on our driving boat, I saw your brother,
Most provident in peril, bind himself,
Courage and hope both teaching him the practise,
To a strong mast that lived upon the sea;
Where, like Arion on the dolphin's back,
I saw him hold acquaintance with the waves
So long as I could see.

*True, madam: and to comfort you with how likely it is, Be reassured, after our ship split,
When you and the too-small number saved with you
Hung onto our lifeboat, I saw your brother,
Very wise and practical in danger, tying himself,
Courage and hope both inspiring him to do so,
To a strong mast that floated on the sea;
Where, like that mythical character riding the dolphin
I saw him fight against the waves
As long as I could see him.*

VIOLA
For saying so, there's gold:
Mine own escape unfoldeth to my hope,
Whereto thy speech serves for authority,
The like of him. Know'st thou this country?

*For saying so, here's some gold:
My own escape encourages the hope,
Which your speech gives authority to,
The likelihood of him living. Do you know this country?*

Captain
Ay, madam, well; for I was bred and born
Not three hours' travel from this very place.

*Yes, madam, well; for I was born and raised
Less that three hours' travel from this very*

VIOLA
Who governs here?

Captain
A noble duke, in nature as in name.

VIOLA
What is the name?

Captain
Orsino.

VIOLA
Orsino! I have heard my father name him:
He was a bachelor then.

Captain
And so is now, or was so very late;
For but a month ago I went from hence,
And then 'twas fresh in murmur,--as, you know,
What great ones do the less will prattle of,--
That he did seek the love of fair Olivia.

VIOLA
What's she?

Captain
A virtuous maid, the daughter of a count
That died some twelvemonth since, then leaving her
In the protection of his son, her brother,
Who shortly also died: for whose dear love,
They say, she hath abjured the company
And sight of men.

VIOLA
O that I served that lady
And might not be delivered to the world,
Till I had made mine own occasion mellow,
What my estate is!

Captain
That were hard to compass;
Because she will admit no kind of suit,

place.

Who rules here?

A noble duke, who is also a good man.

What is the name?

Orsino.

*Orsino! I have heard my father speak of him:
He was a bachelor then.*

*And also is now, or was so very recently;
For it was only a month ago when I left here,
And then the rumor was - since, as you know,
The poor love to gossip about the rich, -
That he wanted the love of beautiful Olivia.*

What is she?

*A virtuous young woman, the daughter of a count That died about a year ago, then leaving her
Under the guardianship of his son, her brother,
Who soon also died; and for whose sake, They say, she has given up the company
And presence of men.*

*Oh how I wish I served that lady
And would not have to face the world,
Until I had helped resolve this situation
And found my fortune!*

*The duke's situation is difficult;
Because she refuses any kind of courting,*

No, not the duke's.

VIOLA
There is a fair behavior in thee, captain;
And though that nature with a beauteous wall
Doth oft close in pollution, yet of thee
I will believe thou hast a mind that suits
With this thy fair and outward character.
I prithee, and I'll pay thee bounteously,
Conceal me what I am, and be my aid
For such disguise as haply shall become
The form of my intent. I'll serve this duke:
Thou shall present me as an eunuch to him:
It may be worth thy pains; for I can sing
And speak to him in many sorts of music
That will allow me very worth his service.
What else may hap to time I will commit;
Only shape thou thy silence to my wit.

Captain
Be you his eunuch, and your mute I'll be:
When my tongue blabs, then let mine eyes not see.

VIOLA
I thank thee: lead me on.

No, not the duke's.

You are both handsome and honest, captain;
And though nature often uses an attractive wall
To disguise trash, yet when it comes to you
I will believe you have a mind that suits
Your attractive and kind appearance.
I ask you, and I'll pay you well,
Hide what I am, and help me
With the kind of disguise that would be helpful
For my purposes. I'll work for this duke:
You can present me as a eunuch to him:
It may be worth your trouble; for I can sing
And talk to him pleasantly and cleverly
That will make him hiring me very worthwhile.
What else may happen I leave to time;
Only keep my secret.

You be his eunuch, and I won't say a thing about it;
If I blab, may I go blind.

Thank you: now show me the way.

Exeunt

SCENE III. OLIVIA'S house.

Enter SIR TOBY BELCH and MARIA

SIR TOBY BELCH
What a plague means my niece, to take the death of
her brother thus? I am sure care's an enemy to life.

*What in tarnation is my niece doing, to react to the death of
her brother in such a way? I am sure moping is bad for you.*

MARIA
By my troth, Sir Toby, you must come in earlier o'
nights: your cousin, my lady, takes great exceptions to your ill hours.

*Truthfully, Sir Toby, you must come in earlier at night: your relative, my lady, has a lot of
issues with your bad timing.*

SIR TOBY BELCH
Why, let her except, before excepted.

Well, let her have issues before she is issued.

MARIA
Ay, but you must confine yourself within the modest
limits of order.

*Yes, but you must keep yourself inside the bounds
of proper behavior.*

SIR TOBY BELCH
Confine! I'll confine myself no finer than I am:
these clothes are good enough to drink in; and so be
these boots too: an they be not, let them hang themselves in their own straps.

*Keep myself! I'll keep myself no better than I am kept: these clothes are good enough to drink it;
and so are
these books too: and if they are not, let them hang themselves in their own straps.*

MARIA
That quaffing and drinking will undo you: I heard
my lady talk of it yesterday; and of a foolish
knight that you brought in one night here to be her wooer.

*That drinking and guzzling will ruin you: I heard
my lady talk of it yesterday; and of that foolish knight that you brought in one night to try and court her.*

SIR TOBY BELCH
Who, Sir Andrew Aguecheek?

Who, Sir Andrew Aguecheek?

MARIA
Ay, he.

Yes, him.

SIR TOBY BELCH

He's as tall a man as any's in Illyria.	*He's as tall as any man in Illyria.*
MARIA What's that to the purpose?	*What's the good of that?*
SIR TOBY BELCH Why, he has three thousand ducats a year.	*Why, he earns three thousand ducats a year [that's a lot of money].*
MARIA Ay, but he'll have but a year in all these ducats: he's a very fool and a prodigal.	*Yes, but he'll only have a year in all these ducats: he's a fool and frivolous.*
SIR TOBY BELCH Fie, that you'll say so! he plays o' the viol-de-gamboys, and speaks three or four languages word for word without book, and hath all the good gifts of nature.	*Nonsense! He plays the violin, and speaks three or four languages without having to consult a book, and has all the good talents anyone could ask for.*
MARIA He hath indeed, almost natural: for besides that he's a fool, he's a great quarreller: and but that he hath the gift of a coward to allay the gust he hath in quarrelling, 'tis thought among the prudent he would quickly have the gift of a grave.	*He is talented indeed: because he's also a fool, he gets into fights: and except for him being too much of a coward to really do all the fighting he wants, it is thought among the more careful that he would quickly get himself killed.*
SIR TOBY BELCH By this hand, they are scoundrels and subtractors that say so of him. Who are they?	*By this hand, only terrible people would say these things of him. Who are they?*
MARIA They that add, moreover, he's drunk nightly in your company.	*They that add, also, that he gets drunk every night with you.*
SIR TOBY BELCH With drinking healths to my niece: I'll drink to her as long as there is a passage in my throat and drink in Illyria: he's a coward and a coystrill that will not drink to my niece till his brains turn o' the toe like a parish-top. What, wench! Castiliano vulgo! for here comes Sir Andrew Agueface.	*Toasting my niece: I'll drink in honor of her as long as there is space in my throat and drink in Illyria: he's a coward and a dishonorable man that will not drink to my niece until his brains turn inside out on themselves with drunkenness. Woman! Enough now! For here comes Sir Andrew Agueface.*

Enter SIR ANDREW

SIR ANDREW
Sir Toby Belch! how now, Sir Toby Belch!

Sir Toby Belch! How are things, Sir Toby Belch?

SIR TOBY BELCH
Sweet Sir Andrew!

Sweet Sir Andrew!

SIR ANDREW
Bless you, fair shrew.

Bless you, lovely lady.

MARIA
And you too, sir.

And you want this too, sir.

SIR TOBY BELCH
Accost, Sir Andrew, accost.

Interrupt, Sir Andrew, interrupt.

SIR ANDREW
What's that?

What is that?

SIR TOBY BELCH
My niece's chambermaid.

My niece's personal maid.

SIR ANDREW
Good Mistress Accost, I desire better acquaintance.

Good Miss Accost, I want to get to know you better.

MARIA
My name is Mary, sir.

My name is Mary, sir.

SIR ANDREW
Good Mistress Mary Accost,--

Good Miss Mary Accost, -

SIR TOBY BELCH
You mistake, knight; 'accost' is front her, board her, woo her, assail her.

You're confused, knight; 'accost' means to front her, board her, woo her, go after her.

SIR ANDREW
By my troth, I would not undertake her in this company. Is that the meaning of 'accost'?

Truthfully, I would not undertake her right here and right now. Is that the meaning of 'accost'?

MARIA
Fare you well, gentlemen.

Farewell, gentlemen.

SIR TOBY BELCH
An thou let part so, Sir Andrew, would thou

If you're going to be difficult, Sir Andrew, I wish

mightst
never draw sword again.

SIR ANDREW
An you part so, mistress, I would I might never draw sword again. Fair lady, do you think you have
fools in hand?

MARIA
Sir, I have not you by the hand.

SIR ANDREW
Marry, but you shall have; and here's my hand.

MARIA
Now, sir, 'thought is free:' I pray you, bring your hand to the buttery-bar and let it drink.

SIR ANDREW
Wherefore, sweet-heart? what's your metaphor?

MARIA
It's dry, sir.

SIR ANDREW
Why, I think so: I am not such an ass but I can keep my hand dry. But what's your jest?

MARIA
A dry jest, sir.

SIR ANDREW
Are you full of them?

MARIA
Ay, sir, I have them at my fingers' ends: marry, now I let go your hand, I am barren.

SIR TOBY BELCH
O knight thou lackest a cup of canary: when did I
see thee so put down?

SIR ANDREW

*you would
never draw your sword again.*

*If you leave like that, Miss, I hope I would never draw my sword again. Beautiful lady, do you think you have
fools that you are dealing with?*

Sir, I do not have you by the hand.

By Mary, but you shall have; and here's my hand.

Now, sir, 'thought is free:' please, bring your hand to bar and let it drink.

Why, sweetheart? What kind of humor are you using?

It is dry [as in deadpan] sir.

Why, I think so: I am not such an ass that I can't keep my hand dry. But what's your joke?

A dry joke, sir.

Are you full of jokes?

Yes, sir, I have them at the tips of my fingers: by Mary, now that I let go of your hand, I am done.

Exit

*Oh knight you're without anything to say: when did I
ever see you so put down?*

Never in your life, I think; unless you see canary put me down. Methinks sometimes I have no more wit
than a Christian or an ordinary man has: but I am a
great eater of beef and I believe that does harm to my wit.

*Never in your life, I think; unless you see a canary put me down. Sometimes I think I have no more intelligence
than any ordinary person has: but I am a glutton and I believe that ruins me.*

SIR TOBY BELCH
No question.

No question.

SIR ANDREW
An I thought that, I'd forswear it. I'll ride home Tomorrow, Sir Toby.

And having said that, I'll confirm it. I'll ride home Tomorrow, Sir Toby.

SIR TOBY BELCH
Pourquoi, my dear knight?

Pourquoi ("why" in French) my dear knight?

SIR ANDREW
What is 'Pourquoi'? do or not do? I would I had bestowed that time in the tongues that I have in fencing, dancing and bear-baiting: O, had I but followed the arts!

What is 'Pourquoi'? Do or not do? I wish that I had used the time studying languages that I have in fencing, dancing, and watching bears fight dogs: oh, if only I had studied the arts!

SIR TOBY BELCH
Then hadst thou had an excellent head of hair.

Then you would have had an excellent head of hair.

SIR ANDREW
Why, would that have mended my hair?

Why, would that have fixed my hair?

SIR TOBY BELCH
Past question; for thou seest it will not curl by nature.

Definitely; for you see it will not curl naturally [he's making a pun about 'artificial' as opposed to 'natural'].

SIR ANDREW
But it becomes me well enough, does't not?

But it looks good enough on me, doesn't it?

SIR TOBY BELCH
Excellent; it hangs like flax on a distaff; and I hope to see a housewife take thee between her legs
and spin it off.

that's kinda gay Toby

*Excellent; it hangs like spinning fiber on a wheel; and I hope to see a housewife take you between her legs
and twist it off.*

SIR ANDREW
Faith, I'll home to-morrow, Sir Toby: your niece

By my faith, I'll go home tomorrow, Sir Toby:

will not be seen; or if she be, it's four to one she'll none of me: the count himself here hard by woos her.

SIR TOBY BELCH
She'll none o' the count: she'll not match above her degree, neither in estate, years, nor wit; I have heard her swear't. Tut, there's life in't, man.

SIR ANDREW
I'll stay a month longer. I am a fellow o' the strangest mind i' the world; I delight in masques and revels sometimes altogether.

SIR TOBY BELCH
Art thou good at these kickshawses, knight?

SIR ANDREW
As any man in Illyria, whatsoever he be, under the
degree of my betters; and yet I will not compare with an old man.

SIR TOBY BELCH
What is thy excellence in a galliard, knight?

SIR ANDREW
Faith, I can cut a caper.

SIR TOBY BELCH
And I can cut the mutton to't.

SIR ANDREW
And I think I have the back-trick simply as strong
as any man in Illyria.

SIR TOBY BELCH
Wherefore are these things hid? wherefore have these gifts a curtain before 'em? are they like to take dust, like Mistress Mall's picture? why dost thou not go to church in a galliard and come home in
a coranto? My very walk should be a jig; I would not

your niece refuses to be seen; or if she does become willing, it's more than likely she'll not want me: the count himself here is courting her hard.

She doesn't want the count: she refuses to marry above her level, not in wealth, age, or intelligence; I have heard her swear it. Tut, there's still hope for you, man.

I'll stay a month longer. I am a man of the strangest mind in the world; I delight in plays and dances and parties all the time.

Are you any good at these pastimes, knight?

*As any man in Illyria, whatever he is, under the level of those better than me; and yet I will not compete
with an old man.*

What is your particular talent, knight?

By my faith, I can dance.

And I can compete with that.

And I think I can do gymnastics simply as strong as any man in Illyria.

*Why are these things hidden? Why do these gifts have a curtain before them? Are they meant to gather dust? Why do
You not dance your way to church and come home in
glory? My very walk should be a jig; I would not so much urinate but in a fountain. What*

so much as make water but in a sink-a-pace. What dost thou mean? Is it a world to hide virtues in? I did think, by the excellent constitution of thy leg, it was formed under the star of a galliard.

SIR ANDREW
Ay, 'tis strong, and it does indifferent well in a flame-coloured stock. Shall we set about some revels?

SIR TOBY BELCH
What shall we do else? were we not born under Taurus?

SIR ANDREW
Taurus! That's sides and heart.

SIR TOBY BELCH
No, sir; it is legs and thighs. Let me see the caper; ha! higher: ha, ha! excellent!

do you mean? Is the world meant for hiding virtues?
I did think, by the excellent structure of your legs, that they were meant for dancing.

Yes, my legs are strong, and they do well in bright clothing. Shall we go about having some fun?

What else we should do? Weren't we born under the sign of Taurus?

Taurus [as in the zodiac sign]! That gives me heart.

Let me see the leap; ha! higher: ha, ha! excellent!

Exeunt

SCENE IV. DUKE ORSINO's palace.

Enter VALENTINE and VIOLA in man's attire

VALENTINE
If the duke continue these favours towards you, Cesario, you are like to be much advanced: he hath
known you but three days, and already you are no stranger.

VIOLA
You either fear his humour or my negligence, that
you call in question the continuance of his love:
is he inconstant, sir, in his favours?

VALENTINE
No, believe me.

VIOLA
I thank you. Here comes the count.

DUKE ORSINO
Who saw Cesario, ho?

VIOLA
On your attendance, my lord; here.

DUKE ORSINO
Stand you a while aloof, Cesario,
Thou know'st no less but all; I have unclasp'd
To thee the book even of my secret soul:
Therefore, good youth, address thy gait unto her;
Be not denied access, stand at her doors,
And tell them, there thy fixed foot shall grow
Till thou have audience.

VIOLA
Sure, my noble lord,
If she be so abandon'd to her sorrow
As it is spoke, she never will admit me.

---

*If the duke continues these favors towards you, Cesario, you are likely to be highly promoted: he has
only known you for three days, and already you are no stranger.*

*You either fear his changing his mind or me no longer doing well, that makes you
question the continuing of his love:
is he inconsistent, sir, in his favors?*

No, believe me.

Thank you. Here comes the count.

Enter DUKE ORSINO, CURIO, and Attendants

Who saw Cesario, hm?

Serving you, sir; here.

*Stand away for a bit, Cesario,
You know nothing less than everything; I have revealed To you even the book of my secret soul:
Therefore, good young man, walk to her;
Do not be denied access to her, stand at her doors,
And tell them that you will stand there
Until she will see you.*

*Sure, my noble lord,
If she is so full of sadness
As it is said, she will never let me in.*

DUKE ORSINO
Be clamorous and leap all civil bounds
Rather than make unprofited return.

VIOLA
Say I do speak with her, my lord, what then?

DUKE ORSINO
O, then unfold the passion of my love,
Surprise her with discourse of my dear faith:
It shall become thee well to act my woes;
She will attend it better in thy youth
Than in a nuncio's of more grave aspect.

VIOLA
I think not so, my lord.

DUKE ORSINO
Dear lad, believe it;
For they shall yet belie thy happy years,
That say thou art a man: Diana's lip
Is not more smooth and rubious; thy small pipe
Is as the maiden's organ, shrill and sound,
And all is semblative a woman's part.
I know thy constellation is right apt
For this affair. Some four or five attend him;
All, if you will; for I myself am best
When least in company. Prosper well in this,
And thou shalt live as freely as thy lord,
To call his fortunes thine.

VIOLA
I'll do my best
To woo your lady:

yet, a barful strife!
Whoe'er I woo, myself would be his wife.

*Be loud and rude
Rather than return empty-handed.*

So if I do speak with her, sir, what then?

*Oh, then explain to her the depth of my love,
Surprise her with an explanation of my devotion: It will be good for you to help my troubles; She will react to it better from someone young Than from an older suitor.*

I do not think so, sir.

*Dear boy, believe it;
For they will still be tricked by your youth,
That say you are a man: Diana's lip
Is not more smooth and plump; your slender throat Is like a young lady's, high-pitched and strong, And everything is like a woman's.
I know your destiny is meant
For this business. Some for or five of you help him; All, if you wish; for myself am best
When I am alone. Do well in this,
And you will live as freely as your lord,
To call his fortunes yours.*

*I'll do my best
To romance your lady:
Aside
Oh, but such trouble and distress!
I am now in love with him myself.*

Exeunt

SCENE V. OLIVIA'S house.

Enter MARIA and Clown

MARIA
Nay, either tell me where thou hast been, or I will
not open my lips so wide as a bristle may enter in
way of thy excuse: my lady will hang thee for thy absence.

No, either tell me where you have been, or I will not open my lips even wide enough for a hair in giving you an excuse: my lady will hang you for your absence.

Clown
Let her hang me: he that is well hanged in this
world needs to fear no colours.

Let her hang me: he that is well hanged in this world does not need to fear any colors.

MARIA
Make that good.

Explain that.

Clown
He shall see none to fear.

He shall have nothing to fear.

MARIA
A good lenten answer: I can tell thee where that
saying was born, of 'I fear no colours.'

A good solid answer: I can tell you where that saying came from, the one of 'I fear no colors.'

Clown
Where, good Mistress Mary?

Where, good Mistress Mary?

MARIA
In the wars; and that may you be bold to say in
your foolery.

In the wars; and it is very risky of you to say it.

Clown
Well, God give them wisdom that have it; and those
that are fools, let them use their talents.

*Well, may God give wise people wisdom, and for those
that are fools, let them use their other abilities.*

MARIA
Yet you will be hanged for being so long absent; or,
to be turned away, is not that as good as a hanging to you?

*Yet you will be hanged for being gone for so long; or
being fired, is that not as good as a hanging to you?*

Clown

Many a good hanging prevents a bad marriage; and,
for turning away, let summer bear it out.

MARIA
You are resolute, then?

Clown
Not so, neither; but I am resolved on two points.

MARIA
That if one break, the other will hold; or, if both break, your gaskins fall.

Clown
Apt, in good faith; very apt. Well, go thy way; if Sir Toby would leave drinking, thou wert as witty a
piece of Eve's flesh as any in Illyria.

MARIA
Peace, you rogue, no more o' that. Here comes my
lady: make your excuse wisely, you were best.

Clown
Wit, an't be thy will, put me into good fooling! Those wits, that think they have thee, do very oft
prove fools; and I, that am sure I lack thee, may pass for a wise man: for what says Quinapalus?

'Better a witty fool, than a foolish wit.'

God bless thee, lady!

OLIVIA
Take the fool away.

Clown
Do you not hear, fellows? Take away the lady.

OLIVIA

---

*Many good hangings prevent bad marriages; and,
as for being fired, let the summer weather take care of me.*

You are decided, then?

No, I am not; but I have resolved two points.

That if one breaks, the other will hold on; or, if both break, you will fall.

*Appropriate, indeed; very approriate. Well, go your way; if Sir Toby gave up drinking, you were as witty a
woman as any in Illyria.*

Quiet, you rogue, enough of that. Here comes my lady: excuse yourself well, you're the best one to do it.

Exit

*Wit, as it is up to you, make me a good fool! Those witty people, that think they have you, very often
turn out to be fools; and I, that am sure I do not have you, may pass for a wise man; for what does Quinapalus say?*

Enter OLIVIA with MALVOLIO

God bless you, lady!

Take the fool away.

Don't you hear, gentlemen? Take away the lady.

Go to, you're a dry fool; I'll no more of you: besides, you grow dishonest.

Clown
Two faults, madonna, that drink and good counsel
will amend: for give the dry fool drink, then is the fool not dry: bid the dishonest man mend himself; if he mend, he is no longer dishonest; if he cannot, let the botcher mend him. Any thing that's mended is but patched: virtue that transgresses is but patched with sin; and sin that amends is but patched with virtue. If that this simple syllogism will serve, so; if it will not, what remedy? As there is no true cuckold but calamity, so beauty's a flower. The lady bade take
away the fool; therefore, I say again, take her away.

OLIVIA
Sir, I bade them take away you.

Clown
Misprision in the highest degree! Lady, cucullus non
facit monachum; that's as much to say as I wear not
motley in my brain. Good madonna, give me leave to
prove you a fool.

OLIVIA
Can you do it?

Clown
Dexterously, good madonna.

OLIVIA
Make your proof.

Clown
I must catechise you for it, madonna: good my mouse
of virtue, answer me.

Enough, you're an unfunny fool; I don't want any more of you: besides, you become dishonest.

Two faults, lady, that drink and good advice will fix: for give the dry fool drink, then the fool is not dry: tell the dishonest man to mend himself; if he mends, he is no longer dishonest; if he cannot, let the butcher mend him. Anything that's mended is simply patched: virtue that does wrong is simply patched with sin; and sin that fixes itself is simply patched with virtue. If that simple logical argument will serve, so; if it will not, what solution is there? As there is no true betrayal but catastrophe, so beauty's a flower. The lady said to take away the fool; therefore, I say again, take her away.

Sir, I told them to take away you.

Inaccuracy in the highest degree! Lady, cucullus non facit monachum; that's as much to say as I am no idiot. Good lady, give me permission to prove you are a fool.

Can you do it?

Skillfully, good lady.

Prove it then.

*I must do so by question and answer, my lady: my good mouse
of good qualities, answer me.*

OLIVIA
Well, sir, for want of other idleness, I'll bide your proof.

Well, sir, since I have nothing else to do, I'll go along with it.

Clown
Good madonna, why mournest thou?

Good lady, why are you mourning?

OLIVIA
Good fool, for my brother's death.

Good fool, I mourn my brother's death.

Clown
I think his soul is in hell, madonna.

I think his soul is in Hell, my lady.

OLIVIA
I know his soul is in heaven, fool.

I know his soul has gone to heaven, fool.

Clown
The more fool, madonna, to mourn for your brother's
soul being in heaven. Take away the fool, gentlemen.

*Then you are a fool, lady, to mourn for your brother's
soul having gone to heaven. Take away the fool, gentlemen.*

OLIVIA
What think you of this fool, Malvolio? doth he not mend?

What do you think of this fool, Malvolio? Does he improve?

MALVOLIO
Yes, and shall do till the pangs of death shake him:
infirmity, that decays the wise, doth ever make the
better fool.

Yes, and shall do until death comes to him: infirmity, that ruins the wise, always makes the better clown.

Clown
God send you, sir, a speedy infirmity, for the better increasing your folly! Sir Toby will be sworn that I am no fox; but he will not pass his word for two pence that you are no fool.

*May God make you old then, and quickly, so that
you will become a fool more quickly too! Sir Toby will swear that I am no fox; but he will not claim that you are no fool.*

OLIVIA
How say you to that, Malvolio?

What do you say to that, Malvolio?

MALVOLIO
I marvel your ladyship takes delight in such a

I am amazed that your ladyship is delighted by

barren rascal: I saw him put down the other day with an ordinary fool that has no more brain than a stone. Look you now, he's out of his guard
already; unless you laugh and minister occasion to
him, he is gagged. I protest, I take these wise men,
that crow so at these set kind of fools, no better than the fools' zanies.

OLIVIA
Oh, you are sick of self-love, Malvolio, and taste
with a distempered appetite. To be generous, guiltless and of free disposition, is to take those things for bird-bolts that you deem cannon-bullets:
there is no slander in an allowed fool, though he do
nothing but rail; nor no railing in a known discreet
man, though he do nothing but reprove.

Clown
Now Mercury endue thee with leasing, for thou speakest well of fools!

MARIA
Madam, there is at the gate a young gentleman much
desires to speak with you.

OLIVIA
From the Count Orsino, is it?

MARIA
I know not, madam: 'tis a fair young man, and well attended.

OLIVIA
Who of my people hold him in delay?

MARIA
Sir Toby, madam, your kinsman.

---

such a unfunny rascal: I saw him put down the other day by an ordinary fool that had no more brain
than a stone. Look now, he's out of his element already; unless you laugh and give him purpose, he is gagged. I protest, I consider these wise men,
that laugh like this and these kinds of fools, no better
than the fools' antics.

Oh, you are sick with self-love, Malvolio, and taste
with a sick person's appetite. To be gnerous, guiltless, and free-spirited, is like taking those things as little pellet strikes that you consider cannon bullets:
there is no false insult in an allowed fool, though he does
nothing but rant; nor no ranting in a known discreet
man, though he does nothing but criticize.

Now Mercury grant you blessings, for you speak well of fools!

Re-enter MARIA

Madam, there is at the gate a young gentleman who very much
wants to speak with you.

Did Count Orsino send him?

I do not know, madam: it is a handsome young man, with several servants.

Which of my people are delaying him?

Sir Toby, madam, your relative.

OLIVIA
Fetch him off, I pray you; he speaks nothing but madman: fie on him!

Get rid of him, please; he says nothing but nonsense: enough with him!

Exit MARIA

Go you, Malvolio: if it be a suit from the count, I
am sick, or not at home; what you will, to dismiss it.

*Go on, Malvolio: if it is a proposal from the count, I
am sick, or not at home; say whatever you want to get rid of it.*

Exit MALVOLIO

Now you see, sir, how your fooling grows old, and
people dislike it.

*Now you see, sir, how your joking gets old, and
people don't like it.*

Clown
Thou hast spoke for us, madonna, as if thy eldest
son should be a fool; whose skull Jove cram with
brains! for,--here he comes,--one of thy kin has a
most weak pia mater.

*You have spoken for us, madam, as if your oldest
son will turn out to be a bool; whose son Jove crams with
brains! For - here he comes - one of your family has a
very weak head.*

Enter SIR TOBY BELCH

OLIVIA
By mine honour, half drunk. What is he at the gate, cousin?

By my honor, half drunk. What is he who is at the gate, relative?

SIR TOBY BELCH
A gentleman.

OLIVIA
A gentleman! what gentleman?

SIR TOBY BELCH
'Tis a gentle man here--a plague o' these pickle-herring! How now, sot!

It is a gentle man here - I'm sick of these [insult]! And what's going on with you, idiot?

Clown
Good Sir Toby!

OLIVIA

Cousin, cousin, how have you come so early by this lethargy?	*Relative, relative, how are you so drunk this early in the day?*
SIR TOBY BELCH Lechery! I defy lechery. There's one at the gate.	*[Mishearing] Lechery! I am no lech. There's someone at the gate.*
OLIVIA Ay, marry, what is he?	*Yes, by Mary, what is he?*
SIR TOBY BELCH Let him be the devil, an he will, I care not: give me faith, say I. Well, it's all one.	*Let him be the devil, even if he is, I don't care: give me faith, I say. Well, it's all the same to me.*
	Exit
OLIVIA What's a drunken man like, fool?	*What is a drunken man like, clown?*
Clown Like a drowned man, a fool and a mad man: onedraught above heat makes him a fool; the second mads him; and a third drowns him.	*one drink more than he needs makes him a fool; the second maddens*
OLIVIA Go thou and seek the crowner, and let him sit o' my coz; for he's in the third degree of drink, he's drowned: go, look after him.	*Go and get the doctor, and let him sit with my relative; for he's in the third level of drunkenness, he's drowned: go, take care of him.*
Clown He is but mad yet, madonna; and the fool shall look to the madman.	*He is still only a madman, my lady; and the fool shall look after the madman.*
	Exit
	Re-enter MALVOLIO
MALVOLIO Madam, yond young fellow swears he will speak with you. I told him you were sick; he takes on him to understand so much, and therefore comes to speak with you. I told him you were asleep; he seems to	*Madam, the young man over there swears he will speak with you. I told him you were sick; he said he knew that, and therefore comes to speak with you. I told him you were sleeping; he seems to have also known that beforehand too, and therefore*

have a foreknowledge of that too, and therefore comes to speak with you. What is to be said to him,
lady? he's fortified against any denial.

OLIVIA
Tell him he shall not speak with me.

MALVOLIO
Has been told so; and he says, he'll stand at your door like a sheriff's post, and be the supporter to a bench, but he'll speak with you.

OLIVIA
What kind o' man is he?

MALVOLIO
Why, of mankind.

OLIVIA
What manner of man?

MALVOLIO
Of very ill manner; he'll speak with you, will you or no.

OLIVIA
Of what personage and years is he?

MALVOLIO
Not yet old enough for a man, nor young enough for
a boy; as a squash is before 'tis a peascod, or a cooling when 'tis almost an apple: 'tis with him in standing water, between boy and man. He is very
well-favoured and he speaks very shrewishly; one
would think his mother's milk were scarce out of him.

OLIVIA
Let him approach: call in my gentlewoman.

MALVOLIO

comes to speak with you. What should I say to him,
lady? He has protected himself against any denial.

Tell him he shall not speak with me.

He has been told so; and he says he'll stand at your door like a guarding policeman, or a piece of architecture, but he'll speak with you.

What kind of man is he?

Why, of humanity.

What sort of man?

One with very bad manners; he'll speak with you, whether you like it or not.

How old is he and what is he like?

Not yet old enough to be a man, but no longer young enough to be
a boy; the way a squash is before it is ready to eat, or a flower bud when it is almost an apple: he is in that zone between being a boy and a man. He is very
handsome and speaks very cleverly; you would think
he was barely grown up.

Let him come near: call in my maid.

Gentlewoman, my lady calls.

Maid, my lady calls.

Exit

Re-enter MARIA

OLIVIA
Give me my veil: come, throw it o'er my face.
We'll once more hear Orsino's embassy.

*Give me my veil: come, throw it over my face.
We'll hear from Orsino's representatives again.*

Enter VIOLA, and Attendants

VIOLA
The honourable lady of the house, which is she?

Which one is the honorable lady of the house?

OLIVIA
Speak to me; I shall answer for her.
Your will?

What do you want?

VIOLA
Most radiant, exquisite and unmatchable
beauty,--I
pray you, tell me if this be the lady of the house,
for I never saw her: I would be loath to cast
away
my speech, for besides that it is excellently well
penned, I have taken great pains to con it. Good
beauties, let me sustain no scorn; I am very
comptible, even to the least sinister usage.

*Most brilliant, exquisite, and incomparable
beauty - I
beg you, tell me if this is the lady of the house,
for I never saw her; I would hate to waste
my speech, for besides it being extremely well
written, I have worked very hard at memorizing
it. Good
beauties, don't subject me to bad feelings; I am
easily offended, even with the least sinister
behavior.*

OLIVIA
Whence came you, sir?

Where did you come from, sir?

VIOLA
I can say little more than I have studied, and that
question's out of my part. Good gentle one, give
me
modest assurance if you be the lady of the
house,
that I may proceed in my speech.

*I can't say much more tan what I have studied,
and that question is beyond me. Good gentle
one, give me
some reassurance if you are the lady of the
house,
that I may continue in my speech.*

OLIVIA
Are you a comedian?

Are you joking?

VIOLA
No, my profound heart: and yet, by the very
fangs
of malice I swear, I am not that I play. Are you

*No, my deepest heart: and yet, by the very fangs
of evil, I swear I am not what I seem to be. Are
you*

the lady of the house?

OLIVIA
If I do not usurp myself, I am.

VIOLA
Most certain, if you are she, you do usurp
yourself; for what is yours to bestow is not
yours
to reserve. But this is from my commission: I
will
on with my speech in your praise, and then show
you
the heart of my message.

OLIVIA
Come to what is important in't: I forgive you the
praise.

VIOLA
Alas, I took great pains to study it, and 'tis
poetical.

OLIVIA
It is the more like to be feigned: I pray you,
keep it in. I heard you were saucy at my gates,
and allowed your approach rather to wonder at
you
than to hear you. If you be not mad, be gone; if
you have reason, be brief: 'tis not that time of
moon with me to make one in so skipping a
dialogue.

MARIA
Will you hoist sail, sir? here lies your way.

VIOLA
No, good swabber; I am to hull here a little
longer. Some mollification for your giant, sweet
lady. Tell me your mind: I am a messenger

OLIVIA
Sure, you have some hideous matter to deliver,
when
the courtesy of it is so fearful. Speak your

the lady of the house?

If I do not take over myself, I am.

*Certainly, if you are her, you do take over
yourself; for what is yours to give is not yours
to keep back. But this is from the job I have been
given: I will
continue with my speech praising you, and then
get to
the main part of my message.*

*Come to what is important in your speech: you
may skip the praise.*

*Oh dear, I worked hard to study it, and it's very
poetic.*

*That makes it more likely to be faked: please,
keep it to yourself. I heard you were sassy at my
gates, and allowed you to come in instead so I
could stare at you
rather than hear you. If you are not insane, go
away; if you are reasonable, be brief: I am not
in the
mood to be playing games.*

Will you sail away, sir? This is the way out.

*No, good shipmate, I will stay in this port a little
longer. Some peacemaking for your tall, sweet
lady. Tell me what you want: I am a
messenger.*

*Surely, you have some terrible thing to tell,
when
you are being so outrageously polite. Get to the*

office. | *point.*

VIOLA
It alone concerns your ear. I bring no overture of war, no taxation of homage: I hold the olive in my
hand; my words are as fun of peace as matter.

*That's for your ears only. I bring no declaration of war, no demands: I am here with the olive branch
this is a peaceful matter.*

OLIVIA
Yet you began rudely. What are you? what would you?

Yet you began rudely. What are you? What do you want?

VIOLA
The rudeness that hath appeared in me have I learned from my entertainment. What I am, and what I
would, are as secret as maidenhead; to your ears, divinity, to any other's, profanation.

*The rudeness that has appeared in me I have learned from my studies. What I am, and what I want, are as secret as women's secrets; to your ears,
something divine, to any other's, something obscene.*

OLIVIA
Give us the place alone: we will hear this divinity.

Give us some privacy: I want to hear this "something divine".

Exeunt MARIA and Attendants

Now, sir, what is your text?

Now, sir, what is your message?

VIOLA
Most sweet lady,--

Sweetest lady,--

OLIVIA
A comfortable doctrine, and much may be said of it.
Where lies your text?

An established compliment, and very good too. Where is your message from?

VIOLA
In Orsino's bosom.

In Orsino's chest.

OLIVIA
In his bosom! In what chapter of his bosom?

In his chest! In what part of his chest?

VIOLA
To answer by the method, in the first of his heart.

To continue the metaphor, in the first part of his heart.

OLIVIA

O, I have read it: it is heresy. Have you no more to say?

VIOLA
Good madam, let me see your face.

OLIVIA
Have you any commission from your lord to negotiate
with my face? You are now out of your text: but we will draw the curtain and show you the picture.
Look you, sir, such a one I was this present: is't not well done?

VIOLA
Excellently done, if God did all.

OLIVIA
'Tis in grain, sir; 'twill endure wind and weather.

VIOLA
'Tis beauty truly blent, whose red and white
Nature's own sweet and cunning hand laid on:
Lady, you are the cruell'st she alive,
If you will lead these graces to the grave
And leave the world no copy.

OLIVIA
O, sir, I will not be so hard-hearted; I will give out divers schedules of my beauty: it shall be inventoried, and every particle and utensil labelled to my will: as, item, two lips, indifferent red; item, two grey eyes, with lids to them; item, one neck, one chin, and so forth. Were
you sent hither to praise me?

VIOLA
I see you what you are, you are too proud;
But, if you were the devil, you are fair.
My lord and master loves you: O, such love
Could be but recompensed, though you were crown'd
The nonpareil of beauty!

Oh, I have read it: it is blasphemy. Do you have nothing else to say?

Good madam, please show me your face.

Has your lord commanded you to be able to see my face? You are now out of messages, but we will pull back the curtain and show you the picture.
Look, sir, this is the face I was given, is it Unveiling

Very well done, if God did it all.

It was made well, sir; it will endure wind and weather.

It is a beauty truly made, whose red and white Nature's own sweet and clever hand laid on: Lady, you are the cruellest woman alive, If you will take these wonderful qualities to the grave And have no child to carry on the looks.

Oh, sir, I will not be so cruel; I will give out several descriptions of my beauty: it shall be inventoried, and every part and item labeled in my will: as, item, two lips basically red; item, two grey eyes, with lids on them; item, one neck, on chin, and so on. Were you sent here to praise me?

I see your problem is that you are too proud; But, even if you were the devil, you are beautiful. The Duke Orsino loves you; Oh, such love Could simply be repaid, even if you were crowed
The absolute perfection of beauty!

OLIVIA
How does he love me?

How much does he love me?

VIOLA
With adorations, fertile tears,
With groans that thunder love, with sighs of fire.

*With promises, many fat tears,
With groans of love like thunder, with sighs of fire.*

OLIVIA
Your lord does know my mind; I cannot love him:
Yet I suppose him virtuous, know him noble,
Of great estate, of fresh and stainless youth;
In voices well divulged, free, learn'd and valiant;
And in dimension and the shape of nature
A gracious person: but yet I cannot love him;
He might have took his answer long ago.

*Your lord does know my decision; I cannot love him:
Even though I consider him virtuous, know he is noble, Wealthy, young;
Pleasantly voiced, free, full of learning and courage; And in physical appearance
An attractive person: but yet I cannot love him;
He might have known my answer long ago.*

VIOLA
If I did love you in my master's flame,
With such a suffering, such a deadly life,
In your denial I would find no sense;
I would not understand it.

*If I did love you the way my master does,
Suffering so much because of it,
Your denial would make no sense;
I would not understand it.*

OLIVIA
Why, what would you?

Why, what would you do?

VIOLA
Make me a willow cabin at your gate,
And call upon my soul within the house;
Write loyal cantons of contemned love
And sing them loud even in the dead of night;
Halloo your name to the reverberate hills
And make the babbling gossip of the air
Cry out 'Olivia!' O, You should not rest
Between the elements of air and earth,
But you should pity me!

*Make myself a cabin out of willow wood at your gate, And keep my soul inside the house;
Write loyal poems of condemned love
And sing them loudly even in the middle of the night; Yell your name to the echoing hills
And make the air itself
Shout out, "Olivia!" Oh, you should not rest
Anywhere between the air and the earth,
Without pitying me!*

OLIVIA
You might do much.
What is your parentage?

*You might manage a lot.
What is your family?*

VIOLA
Above my fortunes, yet my state is well:
I am a gentleman.

*More than my fortune, yet I am doing all right:
I am a nobleman.*

OLIVIA

Get you to your lord;
I cannot love him: let him send no more;
Unless, perchance, you come to me again,
To tell me how he takes it. Fare you well:
I thank you for your pains: spend this for me.

VIOLA
I am no fee'd post, lady; keep your purse:
My master, not myself, lacks recompense.
Love make his heart of flint that you shall love;
And let your fervor, like my master's, be
Placed in contempt! Farewell, fair cruelty.

OLIVIA
'What is your parentage?'
'Above my fortunes, yet my state is well:
I am a gentleman.' I'll be sworn thou art;
Thy tongue, thy face, thy limbs, actions and spirit,
Do give thee five-fold blazon: not too fast: soft, soft!
Unless the master were the man. How now!
Even so quickly may one catch the plague?
Methinks I feel this youth's perfections
With an invisible and subtle stealth
To creep in at mine eyes. Well, let it be.
What ho, Malvolio!

MALVOLIO
Here, madam, at your service.

OLIVIA
Run after that same peevish messenger,
The county's man: he left this ring behind him,
Would I or not: tell him I'll none of it.
Desire him not to flatter with his lord,
Nor hold him up with hopes; I am not for him:
If that the youth will come this way to-morrow,
I'll give him reasons for't: hie thee, Malvolio.

MALVOLIO

Go back to your master;
I cannot love him: tell him to send no one else;
Unless, maybe, you come to me again,
To tell me how he takes it. Farewell:
Thank you for your trouble: here is some money.

I am not a mercenary, lady; keep your coins:
My master, not myself, is not getting paid back.
May love turn anyone you love's heart into a stone; And may your passion, like my master's, be Completely rejected! Farewell, beautiful cruelty.

Exit

'What is your family?'
'More than my money, though I am doing all right: I am a a gentleman.' I could swear you are; Your words, you face, your limbs, action and spirit,
Give you five reasons to be liked: not too fast: quiet, quiet!
Unless that actually was Orsino. What now!
Is it possible to fall in love so quickly?
I believe I feel this youth's perfections
Stealthily, invisibly, and subtly
To creep into my eyes. Well, let it be.
Hey, Malvolio!

Re-enter MALVOLIO

Here, madam, I am at your service.

Run after that same badly behaved messenger, The duke's man: he left this ring behind him, Whether I would give in or not: tell him I don't want any of it. I do not want him to flatter his lord, Or give him false hopes; I am not for him: If that young man will come back here tomorrow, I'll give him reasons for it: off you go, Malvolio.

Madam, I will.

Exit

OLIVIA
I do I know not what, and fear to find
Mine eye too great a flatterer for my mind.
Fate, show thy force: ourselves we do not owe;
What is decreed must be, and be this so.

*I don't know what I'll do, and I'm afraid to find
My eye too much a flatterer for my mind.
Fate; show your force: we do not own
ourselves; What must be done is what must be
done.*

Exit

ACT II

SCENE I. The sea-coast.

Enter ANTONIO and SEBASTIAN

ANTONIO
Will you stay no longer? nor will you not that I go with you?

Can't you please stay longer? Or can I go with you? huh - sounds familiar. almost like#...

SEBASTIAN
By your patience, no. My stars shine darkly over me: the malignancy of my fate might perhaps distemper yours; therefore I shall crave of you your
leave that I may bear my evils alone: it were a bad
recompense for your love, to lay any of them on you.

I'm sorry, but no. My luck has been very bad lately, the awfulness of my fate may perhaps ruin yours; therefore I will ask your forgiveness and permission that I may endure my troubles by myself, it would be a bad repayment for your love, to lay any of them on you. Pylades + Orestes?

ANTONIO
Let me yet know of you whither you are bound.

Let me know where you are going.

SEBASTIAN
No, sooth, sir: my determinate voyage is mere extravagancy. But I perceive in you so excellent a
touch of modesty, that you will not extort from me
what I am willing to keep in; therefore it charges me in manners the rather to express myself. You must know of me then, Antonio, my name is Sebastian,
which I called Roderigo. My father was that Sebastian of Messaline, whom I know you have heard
of. He left behind him myself and a sister, both born in an hour: if the heavens had been pleased, would we had so ended! but you, sir, altered that;
for some hour before you took me from the breach of
the sea was my sister drowned.

No, truthfully, sir: my plans are not serious. But I see that you are such a good person, that you will not demand that I tell you what I want to keep to myself: therefore I am obligated to explain things to you. You must know about me, then, Antonio, my name is Sebastian, though I went by Roderigo. My father was that Sebastian from Messaline, whom I know you have heard of. When he died there was just me and a sister, both born in the same hour: if Fate had been kind, we would have died like that too! But you, sir, changed that; for some hour before you saved me from the sea my sister drowned.

ANTONIO
Alas the day!

Oh no!

SEBASTIAN
A lady, sir, though it was said she much resembled
me, was yet of many accounted beautiful: but,
though I could not with such estimable wonder
overfar believe that, yet thus far I will boldly
publish her; she bore a mind that envy could not but
call fair. She is drowned already, sir, with salt
water, though I seem to drown her remembrance
again with more.

A lady, sir, though people said looked a lot like me, was considered beautiful by many: but, though I couldn't very easily believe that, I will not consider it exaggeration to say this of her; she had a mind that anyone could consider brilliant. She is drowned already, sir, with salt water, though I seem to drown my memories of her with more (tears).

ANTONIO
Pardon me, sir, your bad entertainment.

Forgive me, sir, for being such bad comfort.

SEBASTIAN
O good Antonio, forgive me your trouble.

Oh good Antonio, forgive me for troubling you.

ANTONIO
If you will not murder me for my love, let me be your servant.

If you will not reject me for my affection, let me be your servant.

SEBASTIAN
If you will not undo what you have done, that is,
kill him whom you have recovered, desire it not.
Fare ye well at once: my bosom is full of kindness,
and I am yet so near the manners of my mother, that
upon the least occasion more mine eyes will tell
tales of me. I am bound to the Count Orsino's
court: farewell.

If you will not take back what you have done, that is, kill the man you have saved, don't ask for that. Goodbye at once: my heart is full of kindness, and I am still so near the hometown of my mother, that at least once more I will go and do something. I am heading to the Count Orsino's court: farewell.

Exit

ANTONIO
The gentleness of all the gods go with thee!
I have many enemies in Orsino's court,
Else would I very shortly see thee there.
But, come what may, <u>I do adore thee so</u>,
That danger shall seem sport, and I will go.

[handwritten: They seem to be in love.]

The blessings of the gods upon you! I have many enemies at Orsino's court, Or else I would soon see you there soon. But, no matter what, I like you so much, That the danger seems more like fun, and I'll go anyway.

Exit

SCENE II. A street.

Enter VIOLA, MALVOLIO following

MALVOLIO
Were not you even now with the Countess Olivia?

Weren't you with the Countess Olivia just a moment ago?

VIOLA
Even now, sir; on a moderate pace I have since arrived but hither.

Yes, I have walked at a fairly relaxed pace and just arrived here.

MALVOLIO
She returns this ring to you, sir: you might have saved me my pains, to have taken it away yourself.
She adds, moreover, that you should put your lord
into a desperate assurance she will none of him: and one thing more, that you be never so hardy to
come again in his affairs, unless it be to report your lord's taking of this. Receive it so.

She is returning this ring to you, sir: you could have saved me some trouble, to have taken it away yourself.
She adds, in addition, that you should tell your lord
that she has absolutely no interest in him: and also, don't you dare
come back on his business, unless it is to report how your lord reacts to it. Take the ring now.

VIOLA
She took the ring of me: I'll none of it.

She took the ring from me: I don't want it.

MALVOLIO
Come, sir, you peevishly threw it to her; and her will is, it should be so returned: if it be worth stooping for, there it lies in your eye; if not, be it his that finds it.

Come on, sir, you threw it at her, and her decision is that is how it should be returned: if it is worth bending down for, there it is; if not, let him who finds it keep it.

Exit

VIOLA
I left no ring with her: what means this lady?
Fortune forbid my outside have not charm'd her!
She made good view of me; indeed, so much,
That sure methought her eyes had lost her tongue,
For she did speak in starts distractedly.
She loves me, sure; the cunning of her passion
Invites me in this churlish messenger.
None of my lord's ring! why, he sent her none.
I am the man: if it be so, as 'tis,

I left no ring with her: what does this lady mean? I hope she hasn't fallen for my good looks! She took a long look at me; indeed, so much, That I thought for sure she had lost her train of thought,
For she spoke in a very distracted way.
She loves me, surely; the cleverness of her passion Is teasing me with this rude messenger. She doesn't want my lord's ring! Why, he sent her none. I am the man: if it is so, as it is,

Poor lady, she were better love a dream.
Disguise, I see, thou art a wickedness,
Wherein the pregnant enemy does much.
How easy is it for the proper-false
In women's waxen hearts to set their forms!
Alas, our frailty is the cause, not we!
For such as we are made of, such we be.
How will this fadge? my master loves her dearly;
And I, poor monster, fond as much on him;
And she, mistaken, seems to dote on me.
What will become of this? As I am man,
My state is desperate for my master's love;
As I am woman,--now alas the day!--
What thriftless sighs shall poor Olivia breathe!
O time! thou must untangle this, not I;
It is too hard a knot for me to untie!

Poor lady, she would be better off loving a dream. Disguise, I see, you are a wickedness, In which the devil can do much. How easy it is for the illusion To create an impression in a weak woman's heart! Oh no, our weakness is the cause, not us! For what things make us, that is what we are. How could this be sorted out? My master loves her dearly; And I, poor monster, am just as fond of him; And she, mistaken, seems to be devoted to me. What shall we do? As I seem to be a man, I am desperate for my master's love; As I am a woman, -- curse the day! -- What useless sighs poor Olivia must breathe! Oh time! You must untangle this, not I; It is too difficult a knot for me to untie!

Exit

SCENE III. OLIVIA's house.

Enter SIR TOBY BELCH and SIR ANDREW

SIR TOBY BELCH
Approach, Sir Andrew: not to be abed after midnight is to be up betimes; and 'diluculo surgere,' thou know'st,--

Come on, Sir Andrew: not to be in bed after midnight is to be up on time; and 'diluculo surgere,' you know, --

SIR ANDREW
Nay, my troth, I know not: but I know, to be up late is to be up late.

No, truthfully, I don't know that: but I know, to be up late just means to be up late.

SIR TOBY BELCH
A false conclusion: I hate it as an unfilled can. To be up after midnight and to go to bed then, is early: so that to go to bed after midnight is to go to bed betimes. Does not our life consist of the four elements?

That is incorrect: I hate it as something illogical. To be up after midnight and to then go to bed, is early: so that means going to bed after midnight is to go to bed on time. Doesn't our life consist of the [He means earth, air, fire, and water.]

SIR ANDREW
Faith, so they say; but I think it rather consists of eating and drinking.

By my faith, so they say; but I think it instead consists of eating food and drinking wine and beer.

SIR TOBY BELCH
Thou'rt a scholar; let us therefore eat and drink. Marian, I say! a stoup of wine!

You are a scholar; let us therefore eat and drink. Marian, I'm calling you! Some wine!

Enter Clown

SIR ANDREW
Here comes the fool, i' faith.

Here comes the fool, by my faith.

Clown
How now, my hearts! did you never see the picture
of 'we three'?

*Hello there, gentlemen! Did you never see the picture
of the three of us?*

SIR TOBY BELCH
Welcome, ass. Now let's have a catch.

Welcome, ass. Now let's have a song.

SIR ANDREW
By my troth, the fool has an excellent breast. I had rather than forty shillings I had such a leg, and so sweet a breath to sing, as the fool has. In sooth, thou wast in very gracious fooling last

Truthfully, the fool has a great set of lungs. I would be willing to pay forty shillings to have such legs, and such a great singing voice, as the fool has. In truth, you did a great job of fooling

night, when thou spokest of Pigrogromitus, of the
Vapians passing the equinoctial of Queubus: 'twas
very good, i' faith. I sent thee sixpence for thy leman: hadst it?

last night, when you spoke of Pigrogormitus, of the Vapians passing the equinoctial of Queubus: it was very good, by my faith. I sent you six pence for your tip: did you get it?

SIR TOBY BELCH
Come on; there is sixpence for you: let's have a song.

Come on; here's some money: let's have a song.

SIR ANDREW
There's a testril of me too: if one knight give a--

That's a test of me too: if one knight gives a ---

Clown
Would you have a love-song, or a song of good life?

Would you like a ballad or a drinking song?

SIR TOBY BELCH
A love-song, a love-song.

A ballad, a ballad.

SIR ANDREW
Ay, ay: I care not for good life.

Yes, yes, I don't care about a good life.

Clown
[Sings] O mistress mine, where are you roaming?
O, stay and hear; your true love's coming,
That can sing both high and low:
Trip no further, pretty sweeting;
Journeys end in lovers meeting,
Every wise man's son doth know.

Oh my lady, where are you going
Oh, stay and wait, your true love's coming
Who can sing both high and low:
Wander no further, pretty darling,
Journeys need with lovers meet,
Every wise man and his son knows this.

SIR ANDREW
Excellent good, i' faith.

Extremely good, by my faith.

SIR TOBY BELCH
Good, good.

Good, good.

Clown
[Sings] What is love? 'tis not hereafter;
Present mirth hath present laughter;
What's to come is still unsure:
In delay there lies no plenty;
Then come kiss me, sweet and twenty,

What is love? It is now, not after
Fun now is laughter now;
Who knows what is coming?
In putting things off there is no benefit,
Then come kiss me, sweet twenty-year-old,

Youth's a stuff will not endure. | *Being young is something that will not last.*

SIR ANDREW
A mellifluous voice, as I am true knight. | *A melodious voice, if I am a true knight.*

SIR TOBY BELCH
A contagious breath. | *A catchy tune.*

SIR ANDREW
Very sweet and contagious, i' faith. | *Very sweet and catchy, by my faith.*

Enter MARIA

MARIA
What a caterwauling do you keep here! If my lady
have not called up her steward Malvolio and bid him
turn you out of doors, never trust me.

What wailing are you doing here? If my lady has not called up her steward Malvolio and told him to kick you out, never trush me.

SIR TOBY BELCH
My lady's a Cataian, we are politicians, Malvolio's
a Peg-a-Ramsey, and 'Three merry men be we.' Am not
I consanguineous? am I not of her blood? Tillyvally. Lady!

'There dwelt a man in Babylon, lady, lady!'

My lady is a Catain, we are acting like politicians, Malvolio's spoiling our fun, and we are three jolly men. Oh, we're just having fun! Aren't I her family? Another song, "TIllyvally", Lady!

Sings
'There lived a man in Babylon, lady, lady!'

Clown
Beshrew me, the knight's in admirable fooling. | *My, the knight is doing an excellent job playing the fool.*

SIR ANDREW
Ay, he does well enough if he be disposed, and so do
I too: he does it with a better grace, but I do it more natural.

Yes, he does it well enough if he feels like it, and so do I too: he does it more gracefully, but I do it more naturally.

SIR TOBY BELCH
[Sings] 'O, the twelfth day of December,'-- | *[Sings] 'Oh, the twelfth day of December,'--*

MARIA
For the love o' God, peace! | *Oh, shut up!*

Enter MALVOLIO

MALVOLIO
My masters, are you mad? or what are you? Have ye
no wit, manners, nor honesty, but to gabble like
tinkers at this time of night? Do ye make an
alehouse of my lady's house, that ye squeak out your
coziers' catches without any mitigation or remorse
of voice? Is there no respect of place, persons, nor
time in you?

My masters, have you gone insane? Or what are you? Do you have no sense, manners, or honesty, but to chatter like commoners at this time of night? Are you making a bar out of my lady's house, that you are squeaking your rude songs without any attempt to keep it quiet? Is there no respect of place, people, or time, with you?

SIR TOBY BELCH
We did keep time, sir, in our catches. Sneck up!

We did keep time, sir, in our songs. Keep up!

MALVOLIO
Sir Toby, I must be round with you. My lady bade me
tell you, that, though she harbours you as her
kinsman, she's nothing allied to your disorders. If
you can separate yourself and your misdemeanors, you
are welcome to the house; if not, an it would please
you to take leave of her, she is very willing to bid
you farewell.

Sir Toby, I must be honest with you. My lady told me to tell you that, though she is allowing you to stay as her relative, she has no loyalty to your faults. If you can separate yourself and your bad behavior, you are welcome to the house; if not, go away, she is very willing to tell you goodbye.

SIR TOBY BELCH
'Farewell, dear heart, since I must needs be gone.'

'Farewell, dear heart, since I must leave.'

MARIA
Nay, good Sir Toby.

No, good Sir Toby.

Clown
'His eyes do show his days are almost done.'

'His eyes are showing that his death is near.'

MALVOLIO
Is't even so?

Is that so?

SIR TOBY BELCH
'But I will never die.'

'But I will never die.'

Clown
Sir Toby, there you lie.

Sir Toby, that's a lie.

MALVOLIO
This is much credit to you.

This is a true thing.

SIR TOBY BELCH
'Shall I bid him go?'

"Shall I tell him to go?'

Clown
'What an if you do?'

'And what if you do?'

SIR TOBY BELCH
'Shall I bid him go, and spare not?'

'Shall I tell him to go, without flinching?'

Clown
'O no, no, no, no, you dare not.'

'Oh no no no no, you don't dare to.'

SIR TOBY BELCH
Out o' tune, sir: ye lie. Art any more than a steward? Dost thou think, because thou art virtuous, there shall be no more cakes and ale?

Out of tune, sir: you are lying. Are you any more than a steward? Do you think, because you are virtuous, that there shall be no more food and drink?

Clown
Yes, by Saint Anne, and ginger shall be hot i' themouth too.

Yes, by Saint Anne, and ginger shall be hot in the mouth too.

SIR TOBY BELCH
Thou'rt i' the right. Go, sir, rub your chain with crumbs. A stoup of wine, Maria!

You are correct. Go sir, rub your chain with crumbs. Some wine, Maria!

MALVOLIO
Mistress Mary, if you prized my lady's favour at any
thing more than contempt, you would not give means
for this uncivil rule: she shall know of it, by this hand.

*Madame Mary, if you valued my lady's favor more than
you do, you would not help make possible this rowdy behavior: she shall know about it from me.*

Exit

MARIA
Go shake your ears.

Oh, enough of you.

SIR ANDREW
'Twere as good a deed as to drink when a man's a-hungry, to challenge him the field, and then to

It is as good a deed as to drink when a man is hungry, to challenge him to battle, and then to break promise with him and make a fool of him.

SIR TOBY BELCH
Do't, knight: I'll write thee a challenge: or I'll deliver thy indignation to him by word of mouth.

MARIA
Sweet Sir Toby, be patient for tonight: since the youth of the count's was today with thy lady, she is much out of quiet. For Monsieur Malvolio, let me alone with him: if I do not gull him into a nayword, and make him a common recreation, do not think I have wit enough to lie straight in my bed: I know I can do it.

SIR TOBY BELCH
Possess us, possess us; tell us something of him.

MARIA
Marry, sir, sometimes he is a kind of puritan.

SIR ANDREW
O, if I thought that I'ld beat him like a dog!

SIR TOBY BELCH
What, for being a puritan? thy exquisite reason, dear knight?

SIR ANDREW
I have no exquisite reason for't, but I have reason good enough.

MARIA
The devil a puritan that he is, or any thing that cons state without book and utters it by great crammed, as he thinks, with excellencies, that it is him; and on that vice in him will my revenge

break your promise with him and make a fool out of him.

Do it, knight: I'll write you a challange, or I'll let him know about the challenge by word of mouth.

Good Sir Toby, be patient about tonight; since the servant of the count's was with your lady today, she is in a bad mood. As for Mister Malvolio, leave me alone with him: if I do not trick him and make him the victim of a prank, do not think I am clever enough to lie straight in my bed: I know I can do it.

Explain to us, explain to us: tell us things about him.

By Mary, sir, sometimes he is a bit of a puritan.

Oh, if I thought that I'd beat him like a dog!

What, for being a puritan? What is your excellent reason, my dear knight?

I have no excellent reason for it, but I have a reason good enough.

constantly, but a time-pleaser; an affectioned ass, swarths: the best persuaded of himself, so his grounds of faith that all that look on him love

He is uptight, a showoff, and things way too

find
notable cause to work.

SIR TOBY BELCH
What wilt thou do?

MARIA
I will drop in his way some obscure epistles of love; wherein, by the colour of his beard, the shape
of his leg, the manner of his gait, the expressure of his eye, forehead, and complexion, he shall find
himself most feelingly personated. I can write very
like my lady your niece: on a forgotten matter we
can hardly make distinction of our hands.

SIR TOBY BELCH
Excellent! I smell a device.

SIR ANDREW
I have't in my nose too.

SIR TOBY BELCH
He shall think, by the letters that thou wilt drop, that they come from my niece, and that she's in love with him.

MARIA
My purpose is, indeed, a horse of that colour.

SIR ANDREW
O, 'twill be admirable!

MARIA
Sport royal, I warrant you: I know my physic will
work with him. I will plant you two, and let the fool make a third, where he shall find the letter: fool make a third, where he shall find the letter: observe his construction of it. For this night, to

highly of himself, and it is through that fault of his I will be able to take revenge on him.

What will you do?

I will let him come upon some secret supposed love letters,
which by complimenting the color of his beard, the shape
of his leg, the way of his walking, the expression of his face,
he will find himself very emotionally described. I can write
very like my lady your niece: in fact we have gotten our
handwriting confused before.

Excellent! I smell a great prank.

I have it in my nose too.

He shall think, by the letters that you will drop, that they were written by my niece, and that she's in love with him.

That is basically it, yes.

Oh, that will be amazing!

Much fun, I promise you: I know my strategy will
worth with him. I will position you two, and let the observe his construction of it. For this night, to
watch what he makes of it. But for tonight, go to bed, and dream about the event. Farewell.

bed, and dream on the event. Farewell.

Exit

SIR TOBY BELCH
Good night, Penthesilea.

SIR ANDREW
Before me, she's a good wench.

She's a good woman.

SIR TOBY BELCH
She's a beagle, true-bred, and one that adores me:what o' that?

She's a good woman who adores me, what of it?

SIR ANDREW
I was adored once too.

I once had someone in love with me too.

SIR TOBY BELCH
Let's to bed, knight. Thou hadst need send for more money.

Let's go to bed, knight. You will need to ask for more money.

SIR ANDREW
If I cannot recover your niece, I am a foul way out.

If I can't get your niece to marry me, I will be in bad shape.

SIR TOBY BELCH
Send for money, knight: if thou hast her not i' the end, call me cut.

Send for money, knight: I'm sure you'll get her.

SIR ANDREW
If I do not, never trust me, take it how you will.

If I don't, never trust me, whatever you make of that.

SIR TOBY BELCH
Come, come, I'll go burn some sack; 'tis too late to go to bed now: come, knight; come, knight.

Come, come, I'll go have some more to drink, it is too late to go to bed now: come now, knight, come now, knight.

Exeunt

SCENE IV. DUKE ORSINO's palace.

Enter DUKE ORSINO, VIOLA, CURIO, and others

DUKE ORSINO
Give me some music. Now, good morrow, friends.
Now, good Cesario, but that piece of song,
That old and antique song we heard last night:
Methought it did relieve my passion much,
More than light airs and recollected terms
Of these most brisk and giddy-paced times:
Come, but one verse.

*Give me some music. Now, good day, friends.
Now, my dear Cesario, about that bit of song,
That old traditional song we heard last night:
I thought it made me feel a lot better,
More than the lighter tunes
Of these fast-paced modern times:
Now, just one verse.*

CURIO
He is not here, so please your lordship that should sing it.

He is not here, the man your lordship wanted to sing it.

DUKE ORSINO
Who was it?

CURIO
Feste, the jester, my lord; a fool that the lady Olivia's father took much delight in. He is about the house.

Feste, the jester, my lord; a clown that my lady Olivia's father much enjoyed. He is around the house.

DUKE ORSINO
Seek him out, and play the tune the while.

Go look for him, and play the tune while we wait.

Exit CURIO. Music plays

Come hither, boy: if ever thou shalt love,
In the sweet pangs of it remember me;
For such as I am all true lovers are,
Unstaid and skittish in all motions else,
Save in the constant image of the creature
That is beloved. How dost thou like this tune?

*Come here, boy: if you ever shall love,
In the sweet waves of pain of it remember me; For I am the way that all true lovers are, Unsteady and wavering in all other motions, Except in the constant view of the person That is beloved. How do you like this tune?*

VIOLA
It gives a very echo to the seat
Where Love is throned.

*It gives a perfect echo to the seat
Where Love sits on a throne.*

DUKE ORSINO

Thou dost speak masterly:
My life upon't, young though thou art, thine eye
Hath stay'd upon some favour that it loves:
Hath it not, boy?

VIOLA
A little, by your favour.

DUKE ORSINO
What kind of woman is't?

VIOLA
Of your complexion.

DUKE ORSINO
She is not worth thee, then. What years, i' faith?

VIOLA
About your years, my lord.

DUKE ORSINO
Too old by heaven: let still the woman takeAn elder than herself: so wears she to him,
So sways she level in her husband's heart:
For, boy, however we do praise ourselves,
Our fancies are more giddy and unfirm,
More longing, wavering, sooner lost and worn,
Than women's are.

VIOLA
I think it well, my lord.

DUKE ORSINO
Then let thy love be younger than thyself,
Or thy affection cannot hold the bent;
For women are as roses, whose fair flower
Being once display'd, doth fall that very hour.

VIOLA
And so they are: alas, that they are so;
To die, even when they to perfection grow!

DUKE ORSINO

You speak wisely:
By my life, even though you are young, your eye
Has been upon something that it loves:
Hasn't it, boy?

A little, if you would indulge me.

What kind of woman is she?

Similar in appearance to you.

She is not worth you, then. How old, by my faith?

About as old as you are, my lord.

Someone older that herself: that is how she wears to him,
So that she stays steady in her husband's heart:
For, boy, no matter how much we praise ourselves, Our feelings are more dizzy and unsteady, More intense, more changing, more quickly over Than women's feelings are.

I think it good, my lord.

Then let your love be younger than you,
Or your affection will not be able to last,
For women are like roses, whose beautiful flower Having been once displayed, fall that same hour.

And so they are: what a shame, that they are that way; To die, even when they reach such perfection!

Re-enter CURIO and Clown

O, fellow, come, the song we had last night. Mark it, Cesario, it is old and plain; The spinsters and the knitters in the sun And the free maids that weave their thread with bones Do use to chant it: it is silly sooth, And dallies with the innocence of love, Like the old age.	*Oh, good man, come, sing that song we had last night. Listen, Cesario, it is old and plain; The spinning women and the knitters in the sun And the weaving women Used to chant it: it is silly truth, And speaks of the innocence of love, Like the old age.*
Clown Are you ready, sir?	*Are you ready, sir?*
DUKE ORSINO Ay; prithee, sing.	*Yes, please, sing.*
SONG.	*Music*
Clown Come away, come away, death, And in sad cypress let me be laid; Fly away, fly away breath; I am slain by a fair cruel maid. My shroud of white, stuck all with yew, O, prepare it! My part of death, no one so true Did share it. Not a flower, not a flower sweet On my black coffin let there be strown; Not a friend, not a friend greet My poor corpse, where my bones shall be thrown: A thousand thousand sighs to save, Lay me, O, where Sad true lover never find my grave, To weep there!	*Come away with me, death, And in a coffin let me be laid; Leave me now, leave me now breath; I have been killed by a beautiful cruel young woman. My shroud of white cloth Oh, prepare it! My experience of death, no one so true Shared it. Not a flower, not a sweet flower Be put on my black coffin: Not a friend, not a friend ever visit My poor corpse, where my bones will be thorn: A million sighs to save, Lay me, oh, where No one can ever find my grave, To cry there!*
DUKE ORSINO There's for thy pains.	*Here's for your trouble.*
Clown No pains, sir: I take pleasure in singing, sir.	*No pain, sir: I enjoy singing, sir.*
DUKE ORSINO I'll pay thy pleasure then.	*I'll pay for your pleasure then.*
Clown	

Truly, sir, and pleasure will be paid, one time or another.

DUKE ORSINO
Give me now leave to leave thee.

Clown
Now, the melancholy god protect thee; and the tailor make thy doublet of changeable taffeta, for
thy mind is a very opal. I would have men of such
constancy put to sea, that their business might be
every thing and their intent every where; for that's
it that always makes a good voyage of nothing. Farewell.

DUKE ORSINO
Let all the rest give place.

Once more, Cesario,
Get thee to yond same sovereign cruelty:
Tell her, my love, more noble than the world,
Prizes not quantity of dirty lands;
The parts that fortune hath bestow'd upon her,
Tell her, I hold as giddily as fortune;
But 'tis that miracle and queen of gems
That nature pranks her in attracts my soul.

VIOLA
But if she cannot love you, sir?

DUKE ORSINO
I cannot be so answer'd.

VIOLA
Sooth, but you must.
Say that some lady, as perhaps there is,

Truly, sir, and pleasure will be paid at one time or another.

Give me permission now to leave you.

Now, the gloomy god protect you; and the tailor make your shirt of colorful taffeta, for
your mind is an opal. I wish men of such reliability were put out to sea, so their business could be
everything and their intentions everywhere; for that's
what always makes a good voyage out of nothing. Farewell.

Exit

Everyone else leave us alone.

CURIO and Attendants retire

One more time, Cesario,
Get to such ruling cruelty:
Tell her that my love, more noble than the world,
Better than tons of dirty lands;
The parts that fate has given her,
Tell her, I value as wildly as fortune;
But it is through that miracle and queen of gems That nature gives her, that attracts my soul.

But what if she cannot love you, sir?

I can't accept such an answer.

Truthfully, but you must.
Say that some lady, as maybe there is,

Hath for your love a great a pang of heart
As you have for Olivia: you cannot love her;
You tell her so; must she not then be answer'd?

DUKE ORSINO
There is no woman's sides
Can bide the beating of so strong a passion
As love doth give my heart; no woman's heart
So big, to hold so much; they lack retention
Alas, their love may be call'd appetite,
No motion of the liver, but the palate,
That suffer surfeit, cloyment and revolt;
But mine is all as hungry as the sea,
And can digest as much: make no compare
Between that love a woman can bear me
And that I owe Olivia.

VIOLA
Ay, but I know--

DUKE ORSINO
What dost thou know?

VIOLA
Too well what love women to men may owe:
In faith, they are as true of heart as we.
My father had a daughter loved a man,
As it might be, perhaps, were I a woman,
I should your lordship.

DUKE ORSINO
And what's her history?

VIOLA
A blank, my lord. She never told her love,
But let concealment, like a worm i' the bud,
Feed on her damask cheek: she pined in thought,
And with a green and yellow melancholy
She sat like patience on a monument,
Smiling at grief. Was not this love indeed?

Has for your love such great pains in her heart As you have for Olivia: you cannot love her back;
You tell her so; must she not then accept the answer?

There is no woman's resistance
That can survive the beating of so strong a passion As love gives my heart; no oman's heart
So big, to hold so much; they don't have the capacity
Unfortunately, their love may be called appetite, Not of the stomach, but the palate, That can become full or tired of the same taste; But my love is as hungry as the sea, And can digest as much: do not compare Between the love a woman can have for me And that I have for Olivia.

Yes, but I know -

What do you know?

I know too well what love women may have to men. By my faith, they are as loyal in heart as we. My father had a daughter who loved a man, As it might, possibly, <u>if I were a woman, I would love you.</u>

RIGHT

And what is her story?

A blank page, sir. She never confessed her love, But let the secret, like a worm in the bud, Feed on her health: she wanted him in thought,
And full of gloom
She sat like a monument of patience,
Smiling in her grief. Wasn't this love too?

We men may say more, swear more: but indeed
Our shows are more than will; for still we prove
Much in our vows, but little in our love.

DUKE ORSINO
But died thy sister of her love, my boy?

VIOLA
I am all the daughters of my father's house,
And all the brothers too: and yet I know not.
Sir, shall I to this lady?

DUKE ORSINO
Ay, that's the theme.
To her in haste; give her this jewel; say,
My love can give no place, bide no denay.

We men may say more, promise more, but indeed
What we show is more than what we can do, for still we prove
A lot in our promises, but not much in our love.

But did you sister die of her love, my boy?

I am all the daughters left of my family,
And all the brothers too: and yet I do not know.
Sir, shall I go to the lady?

Yes, that's what I want.
Go to her quickly; give her this jewel; say
My love cannot accept any denial.

Exeunt

SCENE V. OLIVIA's garden.

Enter SIR TOBY BELCH, SIR ANDREW, and FABIAN

SIR TOBY BELCH
Come thy ways, Signior Fabian.

Come this way, Sir Fabian.

FABIAN
Nay, I'll come: if I lose a scruple of this sport, let me be boiled to death with melancholy.

No, I'll come: if I lose even a moment of this fun, let me be boiled to death with gloom.

SIR TOBY BELCH
Wouldst thou not be glad to have the niggardly rascally sheep-biter come by some notable shame?

Wouldn't you be glad to have this miserly and ungenerous rascally sheep-biter come to some noteworthy shame?

FABIAN
I would exult, man: you know, he brought me out o'
favour with my lady about a bear-baiting here.

*I would rejoice, man: you know, he got me in trouble
with my lady about a bear-baiting here.*

SIR TOBY BELCH
Here comes the little villain.

Here comes the [insult].

Enter MARIA

How now, my metal of India!

What's going on now, my jewel?

MARIA
Get ye all three into the box-tree: Malvolio's coming down this walk: he has been yonder i' the
sun practising behavior to his own shadow this half
hour: observe him, for the love of mockery; for I
know this letter will make a contemplative idiot of
him. Close, in the name of jesting! Lie thou there,

*All three of you, hide: Malvolio's coming down this walk: he has been over in the
sun prancing around at his own shadow this past half
hour: watch him, for the love of mockery; for I*

him. Hide, for the sake of the joke! Lie down over there,

Throws down a letter

for here comes the trout that must be

[Ed note: It is actually possible to catch a

caught with tickling.

trout by tickling, but very difficult.]

Exit

Enter MALVOLIO

MALVOLIO
'Tis but fortune; all is fortune. Maria once told me she did affect me: and I have heard herself come
thus near, that, should she fancy, it should be one
of my complexion. Besides, she uses me with a more
exalted respect than any one else that follows her.
What should I think on't?

It is only luck; everything is luck. Maria once told me she did have a fondness for me, and I have heard herself come this close, that, if she did fall in love, it would be someone who looked like me. Besides, she treats me with more high respect than anyone else that follows her.
What should I think of it?

SIR TOBY BELCH
Here's an overweening rogue!

Here's a preening jerk!

FABIAN
O, peace! Contemplation makes a rare turkey-cock
of him: how he jets under his advanced plumes!

Oh, yes! He's such a peacock when he thinks,
look how he dances under his spreading feathers!

SIR ANDREW
'Slight, I could so beat the rogue!

I swear I could beat him in a fight!

SIR TOBY BELCH
Peace, I say.

Quiet, I say.

MALVOLIO
To be Count Malvolio!

Oh if I were Count Malvolio!

SIR TOBY BELCH
Ah, rogue!

[Insult]

SIR ANDREW
Pistol him, pistol him.

Shoot him, shoot him.

SIR TOBY BELCH
Peace, peace!

Quiet, quiet!

MALVOLIO

There is example for't; the lady of the Strachy married the yeoman of the wardrobe.

It's happened before; the lady of the Strachy married one of her servants.

SIR ANDREW
Fie on him, Jezebel!

[More insults and cursing.]

FABIAN
O, peace! now he's deeply in: look how imagination blows him.

Oh, enough! Look how he's deeply in: look how imagination carries him away.

MALVOLIO
Having been three months married to her, sitting in
my state,--

*Having been married to her for three months, sitting in
my splendor,--*

SIR TOBY BELCH
O, for a stone-bow, to hit him in the eye!

Oh, I wish I had a slingshot, to hit him in the eye! [Etc.]

MALVOLIO
Calling my officers about me, in my branched velvet
gown; having come from a day-bed, where I have left
Olivia sleeping,--

Calling my offers around me, in my velvet robes; having come from a bed where I have left Olivia asleep,--

SIR TOBY BELCH
Fire and brimstone!

[More cursing]

FABIAN
O, peace, peace!

Oh quiet, quiet!

MALVOLIO
And then to have the humour of state; and after a
demure travel of regard, telling them I know my
place as I would they should do theirs, to for my
kinsman Toby,--

*And then to be the one in charge; and after a
bunch of them honoring them, telling them I know my
place as I want them to know theirs, so for my
relative Toby,--*

SIR TOBY BELCH
Bolts and shackles!

[More cursing]

FABIAN
O peace, peace, peace! now, now.

Oh quiet, quiet, quiet! Now, now.

MALVOLIO
Seven of my people, with an obedient start, make
out for him: I frown the while; and perchance wind
up watch, or play with my--some rich jewel. Toby
approaches; courtesies there to me,--

Seven of my people, obediently, make their way to him: I frown all the time; and maybe play with some expensive jewel of mine. Toby comes near; bows to me,--

SIR TOBY BELCH
Shall this fellow live?

Should we kill him?

FABIAN
Though our silence be drawn from us with cars, yet peace.

No matter what, quiet.

MALVOLIO
I extend my hand to him thus, quenching my familiar
smile with an austere regard of control,--
Saying, 'Cousin Toby, my fortunes having cast me on
your niece give me this prerogative of speech,'--

I reach my hand out to him like this, keeping down my familiar smile with my dignified control, -- Saying, 'Cousin Toby, my fate having brought me to your niece giving me this reason to speak,' --

SIR TOBY BELCH
What, what?

What now?

MALVOLIO
'You must amend your drunkenness.'

'You must control your drunkenness.'

SIR TOBY BELCH
Out, scab!

[More insults.]

FABIAN
Nay, patience, or we break the sinews of our plot.

No, patience, or else we will ruin our plot.

MALVOLIO
'Besides, you waste the treasure of your time with
a foolish knight,'--

'Besides, you waste your valuable time with a silly knight,'--

SIR ANDREW
That's me, I warrant you.

That's me, I bet.

MALVOLIO
'One Sir Andrew,'--   *'That Sir Andrew,'--*

SIR ANDREW
I knew 'twas I; for many do call me fool.   *I knew it was me; because many call me a fool.*

MALVOLIO
What employment have we here?   *What do we have here?*

Taking up the letter

FABIAN
Now is the woodcock near the gin.   *Now the bird is near the trap.*

SIR TOBY BELCH
O, peace! and the spirit of humour intimate reading aloud to him!   *Oh, quiet! And I hope he reads aloud!*

MALVOLIO
By my life, this is my lady's hand these be her very C's, her U's and her T's and thus makes she her great P's. It is, in contempt of question, her hand.   *By my life, this is my lady's handwriting; these are her own C's, her U's and her T's and that's how she makes her large P's. It is, without a doubt, her handwriting.*

SIR ANDREW
Her C's, her U's and her T's: why that?   *Her C's, her U's, and her T's, what is that for?*

MALVOLIO
[Reads] 'To the unknown beloved, this, and my good wishes:'--her very phrases! By your leave, wax. Soft! and the impressure her Lucrece, with which she uses to seal: 'tis my lady. To whom should this be?   *'To the one who does not know I love them, this, and my good wishes:' -- her own ways of writing! By your permission, wax. Soft! And the mark of her ring, with which she It even uses her wax seal! It must be her. To whom is it written?*

FABIAN
This wins him, liver and all.   *He's fallen for it.*

MALVOLIO
[Reads] Jove knows I love:
But who?
Lips, do not move;
No man must know.
'No man must know.' What follows? the numbers   *God knows I love. But who? I must stay silent; No man can know. 'No man can know.' What comes after? The numbers*

altered! 'No man must know:' if this should be thee, Malvolio?

SIR TOBY BELCH
Marry, hang thee, brock!

MALVOLIO
[Reads]I may command where I adore;
But silence, like a Lucrece knife,
With bloodless stroke my heart doth gore:
M, O, A, I, doth sway my life.

FABIAN
A fustian riddle!

SIR TOBY BELCH
Excellent wench, say I.

MALVOLIO
M, O, A, I; this simulation is not as the former: and
yet, to crush this a little, it would bow to me, for
every one of these letters are in my name. Soft!
here follows prose.

'If this fall into thy hand, revolve. In my stars I
am above thee; but be not afraid of greatness: some
are born great, some achieve greatness, and some
have greatness thrust upon 'em. Thy Fates open
their hands; let thy blood and spirit embrace them;
and, to inure thyself to what thou art like to be,
cast thy humble slough and appear fresh. Be
opposite with a kinsman, surly with servants; let
thy tongue tang arguments of state; put

changed! 'No man must no:' if this turns out to be you, Malvolio?

[More curses and insults.]

I may give orders where I love;
But silence, like a sharp dagger,
Bloodlessly stabs at my heart:
M, O, A, I rules my life.

What a great trick!

A great woman, I say.

M,O,A,I; this coded message is not just like earlier,
yet, it seems to be me, because
each one of these letters are in my name. Quiet! there is some prose now.

Reads
Reads aloud.

'If this falls into your hands, change. In my birth I
am above you; but do not be afraid of greatness: some
are born great, some reach greatness, and some
have greatness pushed upon them. Your fate opens
its hands; let your blood and spirit embrace them;
and, to make yourself ready for what you are likely to be,
shed your humble skin and appear fresh. Be
a jerk with a family member, rude with servants; let
you make lots of arguments and get into

thyself into the trick of singularity: she thus advises thee that sighs for thee. Remember who commended thy yellow stockings, and wished to see thee ever cross-gartered: I say, remember. Go to, thou art made, if thou desirest to be so; if not, let me see thee a steward still, the fellow of servants, and not worthy to touch Fortune's fingers. Farewell. She that would alter services with thee, THE FORTUNATE-UNHAPPY.'
Daylight and champaign discovers not more: this is open. I will be proud, I will read politic authors, I will baffle Sir Toby, I will wash off gross acquaintance, I will be point-devise the very man. I do not now fool myself, to let imagination jade me; for every reason excites to this, that my lady loves me. She did commend my yellow stockings of late, she did praise my leg being cross-gartered; and in this she manifests herself to my love, and with a kind of injunction drives me to these habits of her liking. I thank my stars I am happy. I will be strange, stout, in yellow stockings, and cross-gartered, even with the swiftness of putting on. Jove and my stars be praised! Here is yet a postscript.

fights this is her advice, the one that is in love with you. Remember who praised your yellow stockings, and always wanted to see them criss-crossed: I say, remember. Go no, you are made, if you want to be; if not, let me see you still a steward, one of the servants, and not worth of good fortune. Fareell. She that would change her relationship with you, The Lucky-Sad.'
There does not seem to be any more to this letter.
I will be haughty, I will read political authors, I will confuse Sir Toby, I will get rid of casual friendships, I will be in every way the man she wants. I am not fooling myself, to let imagination change me; all the evidence points to this, that my lady loves me. She did praise my recent yellow stockings, she did praise me wearing criss-cross garters; and in this she shows her love for me, and with a kind of command pushes me to these habits that she likes. I thank my lucky stars I am happy. I will act strange, strong, in yellow stockings, and cross-gartered, as soon as I can put them on. Jove and my lucky stars be thanked! Here there is still a P.S.

Reads

'Thou canst not choose but know who I am. If thou
entertainest my love, let it appear in thy smiling;
thy smiles become thee well; therefore in my
presence still smile, dear my sweet, I prithee.'
Jove, I thank thee: I will smile; I will do everything that thou wilt have me.

*You cannot choose to not to know who I am. If you
return my love, let it appear in your smiling;
you look good when you smile; therefore in my
presence smile always, my sweetheart, please.'
Thank Jove: I will smile; I will do everything that you want from me.*

Exit

FABIAN
I will not give my part of this sport for a pension of thousands to be paid from the Sophy.

I would not give up my portion of this fun for even a pension of thousands to be paid from the state bank.

SIR TOBY BELCH
I could marry this wench for this device.

I could marry this woman for this idea.

SIR ANDREW
So could I too.

I could too.

SIR TOBY BELCH
And ask no other dowry with her but such another jest.

And ask no other dowry from her but another joke like this.

SIR ANDREW
Nor I neither.

Me neither.

FABIAN
Here comes my noble gull-catcher.

Here comes my noble prankster.

Re-enter MARIA

SIR TOBY BELCH
Wilt thou set thy foot o' my neck?

Will you put your foot on my neck?

SIR ANDREW
Or o' mine either?

Or on mine either?

SIR TOBY BELCH
Shall I play my freedom at traytrip, and become thy bond-slave?

Shall I get rid of my freedom, and become your slave?

SIR ANDREW
I' faith, or I either?

By my faith, me too?

SIR TOBY BELCH Why, thou hast put him in such a dream, that when the image of it leaves him he must run mad.	*Why, you have put in him such a dream, that when he loses it he must go crazy.*
MARIA Nay, but say true; does it work upon him?	*No, but tell me; is it working?*
SIR TOBY BELCH Like aqua-vitae with a midwife.	*Yes, amazingly well.*
MARIA If you will then see the fruits of the sport, mark his first approach before my lady: he will come to her in yellow stockings, and 'tis a colour she abhors, and cross-gartered, a fashion she detests; and he will smile upon her, which will now be so unsuitable to her disposition, being addicted to a melancholy as she is, that it cannot but turn him into a notable contempt. If you will see it, follow me.	*If you will then see the results of the fun, watch his first approach to my lady: he will come to her in yellow stockings, and it is a color she hates, and cross-gartered, a style she hates; and he will smile at her, which will now be so unsuitable to her preferences, as she is so fond of gloominess, that it can't do anything but turn him into something she hates. If you want to see it, follow me.*
SIR TOBY BELCH To the gates of Tartar, thou most excellent devil of wit!	*I would follow you anywhere!*
SIR ANDREW I'll make one too.	*Me too.* *Exeunt*

ACT III

SCENE I. OLIVIA's garden.

Enter VIOLA, and Clown with a tabour

VIOLA
Save thee, friend, and thy music: dost thou live by
thy tabour?

*Save you, friend, and your music: do you live by
your tabour [a type of musical instrument]?*

Clown
No, sir, I live by the church.

No, sir, I live by the church.

VIOLA
Art thou a churchman?

Are you a church man?

Clown
No such matter, sir: I do live by the church; for
I do live at my house, and my house doth stand by
the church.

*No, no, sir: I do live by the church; for
I live at my house, and my house stands by
the church [he means the actual building].*

VIOLA
So thou mayst say, the king lies by a beggar, if a
beggar dwell near him; or, the church stands by thy
tabour, if thy tabour stand by the church.

*By that logic you may say that a king lies
by a beggar, if a beggar lives near him; or
that the church stands by your
tabour, if your tabour stands by the church.*

Clown
You have said, sir. To see this age! A sentence is
but a cheveril glove to a good wit: how quickly the
wrong side may be turned outward!

*Good point. These times we live in! A sentence is
just a glove over a clever mind: how quickly the
misunderstood meaning may be taken!*

VIOLA
Nay, that's certain; they that dally nicely with
words may quickly make them wanton.

*No, that's certain; those that use words very
precisely will quickly make them wild.*

Clown
I would, therefore, my sister had had no name, sir.

*I would prefer, therefore, that my sister had no
name, sir.*

VIOLA
Why, man?

Why?

Clown
Why, sir, her name's a word; and to dally with that
word might make my sister wanton. But indeed words
are very rascals since bonds disgraced them.

VIOLA
Thy reason, man?

Clown
Troth, sir, I can yield you none without words; and
words are grown so false, I am loath to prove
reason with them.

VIOLA
I warrant thou art a merry fellow and carest for nothing.

Clown
Not so, sir, I do care for something; but in my
conscience, sir, I do not care for you: if that be
to care for nothing, sir, I would it would make you invisible.

VIOLA
Art not thou the Lady Olivia's fool?

Clown
No, indeed, sir; the Lady Olivia has no folly: she
will keep no fool, sir, till she be married; and
fools are as like husbands as pilchards are to
herrings; the husband's the bigger: I am indeed not
her fool, but her corrupter of words.

VIOLA
I saw thee late at the Count Orsino's.

Clown
Foolery, sir, does walk about the orb like the sun,

*Why, sir, her name is a word, and to mess around with that
word might make my sister a hussy. But indeed words
are very rascals since they were disgraced.*

Your reason, man?

*Truthfully sir, I can't give you any without words; and
since words have become so false, I would hate to prove
reason with them.*

I believe you are a cheerful fellow and have no cares.

*No, sir, I do care for something; but in my
conscience, sir, I do not have feelings for you one way or another: if that means
to care for nothing, sir, I wish it would make you invisible.*

Aren't you the Lady Olivia's fool?

*No, indeed, sir, the Lady Olivia has no
foolishness: she will keep no fool, sir, until she
is married; and fools are like husbands the way
pilchards [a kind of small fish] are like
herrings; husbands are bigger ones: I am
indeed not her fool, but her man in charge of wordplay.*

I saw you at the Count Orsino's.

Foolery, sir, walks around the sky like the sun does,

it shines every where. I would be sorry, sir, but
the fool should be as oft with your master as with
my mistress: I think I saw your wisdom there.

VIOLA
Nay, an thou pass upon me, I'll no more with thee.
Hold, there's expenses for thee.

Clown
Now Jove, in his next commodity of hair, send thee a beard!

VIOLA
By my troth, I'll tell thee, I am almost sick for one;
though I would not have it grow on my chin. Is thy
lady within?

CLOWN
My lady is within, sir. I will construe to them whence you
come; who you are and what you would are out of my
welkin, I might say 'element,' but the word is over-worn.

VIOLA
This fellow is wise enough to play the fool;
And to do that well craves a kind of wit:
He must observe their mood on whom he jests,
The quality of persons, and the time,
And, like the haggard, cheque at every feather
That comes before his eye. This is a practise
As full of labour as a wise man's art
For folly that he wisely shows is fit;
But wise men, folly-fall'n, quite taint their wit.

it shines everywhere. I would be sorry, sir, except
The fool should be as often with your master as with
my mistress: I think I saw there how wise you are.

No, leave me alone, I won't deal with you any loner.
Hold, here's some money.

Now may Jove, in his next distribution of hair, send you a beard!

Truthfully, I'll tell you, I am almost sick for Aside
though it would not grow on my chin. Is your
lady inside?

My lady is inside, sir. I will tell them from where you
come; who you are and what you want are out of my
sky, I might say 'element', but the word is overused.

Exit

This fellow is wise enough to act like a fool;
And to do that well requires a kind of intelligence: He must observe the moods of the people he jokes towards,
The nature of people, and the time,
And, like a hatmaker, check carefully every feather
That comes in front of his eye. This is a practice
As full of labor as a wise man's skill
For the follow that he wisely shows fits;
But wise men, when they act as fools, ruin their wit.

Enter SIR TOBY BELCH, and SIR ANDREW

SIR TOBY BELCH
Save you, gentleman.

Good day, gentleman.

VIOLA
And you, sir.

And you too, sir.

SIR TOBY BELCH
Will you encounter the house? my niece is desirous
you should enter, if your trade be to her.

*Will you come into the house? My niece wants
you to enter, if your job is to see her.*

VIOLA
I am bound to your niece, sir; I mean, she is the list of my voyage.

I am required to visit your niece, sir; I mean that is the purpose of my trip.

SIR TOBY BELCH
Taste your legs, sir; put them to motion.

Try your legs, sir; get them moving.

VIOLA
My legs do better understand me, sir, than I understand what you mean by bidding me taste my legs.

My legs do understand me better, sir, than I understand what you mean by telling me to taste my legs.

SIR TOBY BELCH
I mean, to go, sir, to enter.

I mean, go on, sir, enter.

I will answer you with gait and entrance. But we are prevented.

I will answer you with walking and entering. But we are interrupted.

Enter OLIVIA and MARIA

Most excellent accomplished lady, the heavens rain
odours on you!

*Amazing and talented lady, may the heavens rain
fragrances on you!*

SIR ANDREW
That youth's a rare courtier: 'Rain odours;' well.

That youth's an unusual nobleman: 'Rain fragrances;' well.

OLIVIA
Let the garden door be shut, and leave me to my hearing.

Shut the garden door, and leave us alone.

Exeunt SIR TOBY BELCH, SIR ANDREW, and MARIA

Give me your hand, sir.

VIOLA
My duty, madam, and most humble service.

OLIVIA
What is your name?

VIOLA
Cesario is your servant's name, fair princess.

OLIVIA
My servant, sir! 'Twas never merry world
Since lowly feigning was call'd compliment:
You're servant to the Count Orsino, youth.

VIOLA
And he is yours, and his must needs be yours:
Your servant's servant is your servant, madam.

OLIVIA
For him, I think not on him: for his thoughts,
Would they were blanks, rather than fill'd with me!

VIOLA
Madam, I come to whet your gentle thoughts
On his behalf.

OLIVIA
O, by your leave, I pray you,
I bade you never speak again of him:
But, would you undertake another suit,
I had rather hear you to solicit that
Than music from the spheres.

VIOLA
Dear lady,--

OLIVIA
Give me leave, beseech you. I did send,
After the last enchantment you did here,
A ring in chase of you: so did I abuse
Myself, my servant and, I fear me, you:

Give me your hand, sir.

I give you my service humbly, madam.

What's your name?

Cesario is your servant's name, beautiful princess.

My servant, sir! There was never such a silly world Since such pretending was called a compliment: You're a servant to Count Orsino, young man.

And he is yours, and his must also be yours; The servant of your servant is your servant, madam.

For him, I do not think of him: as for his thoughts, If only they were blank, rather than filled with me!

Madam, I come to sharpen your gentle thoughts For his sake.

*Oh please, I beg you,
I told you to never speak of him again:
But if instead you were to do another kind of courting, I would rather hear you do that Than listen to heavenly music.*

My dear lady,--

*Give me permission, please. I did send,
After the last time you were here,
A ring to chase after you: and that's how I abused Myself, my servant, and, I'm*

Under your hard construction must I sit,
To force that on you, in a shameful cunning,
Which you knew none of yours: what might you think?
Have you not set mine honour at the stake
And baited it with all the unmuzzled thoughts
That tyrannous heart can think? To one of your receiving
Enough is shown: a cypress, not a bosom,
Hideth my heart. So, let me hear you speak.

VIOLA
I pity you.

OLIVIA
That's a degree to love.

VIOLA
No, not a grize; for 'tis a vulgar proof,
That very oft we pity enemies.

OLIVIA
Why, then, methinks 'tis time to smile again.
O, world, how apt the poor are to be proud!
If one should be a prey, how much the better
To fall before the lion than the wolf!

The clock upbraids me with the waste of time.
Be not afraid, good youth, I will not have you:
And yet, when wit and youth is come to harvest,
Your were is alike to reap a proper man:
There lies your way, due west.

VIOLA
Then westward-ho! Grace and good disposition

afraid, you: Under your heart heart I must sit, To force that on you, in a shameful trick,
Which you knew was not yours: what did you think?
Have you not set my honor at the stake
And taunted it with all the uncontrolled thoughts
That a dictator of a heart can think? To one of your receiving
Enough is shown: a tree, not a chest,
Hides my heart. So, let me hear you speak.

I feel sorry for you.

That's similar to love.

No, not much; it's not a good proof,
For we very often pity enemies.

Why, then, I think it is time to smile again.
Oh, world, how appropriate the poor are to be proud!
If you have to be a victim, how much better
To fall in front of the lion than the wolf!

Clock strikes

The clock criticizes me with the waste of time.
Do not be afraid, good young man, I will not have you:
And yet, when wit and youth has come to full bloom,
You seem likely to turn out to be a proper man:
Your way is that way, straight west.

Then I shall go west! Grace and good

Attend your ladyship!
You'll nothing, madam, to my lord by me?

OLIVIA
Stay:
I prithee, tell me what thou thinkest of me.

VIOLA
That you do think you are not what you are.

OLIVIA
If I think so, I think the same of you.

VIOLA
Then think you right: I am not what I am.

OLIVIA
I would you were as I would have you be!

VIOLA
Would it be better, madam, than I am?
I wish it might, for now I am your fool.

OLIVIA
O, what a deal of scorn looks beautiful
In the contempt and anger of his lip!
A murderous guilt shows not itself more soon
Than love that would seem hid: love's night is noon.
Cesario, by the roses of the spring,
By maidhood, honour, truth and every thing,
I love thee so, that, maugre all thy pride,
Nor wit nor reason can my passion hide.
Do not extort thy reasons from this clause,
For that I woo, thou therefore hast no cause,
But rather reason thus with reason fetter,
Love sought is good, but given unsought better.

VIOLA
By innocence I swear, and by my youth
I have one heart, one bosom and one truth,
And that no woman has; nor never none
Shall mistress be of it, save I alone.
And so adieu, good madam: never more

---

mood Be with your ladyship!
You have nothing, madam, for me to take to my lord?

Wait:
Please, tell me what you think of me.

That you think you are not what you are.

If that is what I think, I also think that of you.

Then you think correctly: I am not what I am.

I wish you were the way I wish you were!

Would it be better, madam, than I am?
I wish it would, for now I am your fool.

Oh, how his disinterest looks beautiful
In his angry lip!
A murderous guilt does not show itself more soon Than love that would seem hidden: love's night is noon.
Cesario, I swear by the roses of spring,
By my womanhood, by honor, truth, and everything, I love you so, that, no matter all your pride, No cleverness or wisdom can hide my passion. Do not demand me to explain why, For that I woo, you therefore have no cause,
But instead have a better reason,
Love searched for is good, but even freely is better.

By my innocence I swear, and by my youth
I have one heart, one chest and one truth,
Which no woman has, and never one
Shall be the mistress of it, except for me alone. And so farewell, good madam: I will

Will I my master's tears to you deplore.

OLIVIA
Yet come again; for thou perhaps mayst move
That heart, which now abhors, to like his love. *insert keysmash* I have feelings

never again Come tell you of my master's sorrows.

But come again; because you perhaps may begin
To love me the way he does.

Exeunt

SCENE II. OLIVIA's house.

[handwritten: on Dick of y'all]

Enter SIR TOBY BELCH, SIR ANDREW, and FABIAN

SIR ANDREW
No, faith, I'll not stay a jot longer.

No, by my faith, I won't stay a moment longer.

SIR TOBY BELCH
Thy reason, dear venom, give thy reason.

Your reason, dear snake, give you reason.

FABIAN
You must needs yield your reason, Sir Andrew.

You must give us your reason, Sir Andrew.

SIR ANDREW
Marry, I saw your niece do more favours to the
count's serving-man than ever she
bestowed upon me;
I saw't i' the orchard.

*By Mary, I saw your niece give more affection to
the count's serving-man than she ever gave to
me; I saw in the orchard.*

SIR TOBY BELCH
Did she see thee the while, old boy? tell me that.

*Did she see you during that time, old boy? Tell
me that.*

SIR ANDREW
As plain as I see you now.

As clearly as I see you now.

FABIAN
This was a great argument of love in her toward
you.

That is good evidence of her love towards you.

SIR ANDREW
'Slight, will you make an ass o' me?

Are you making fun of me?

FABIAN
I will prove it legitimate, sir, upon the oaths of
judgment and reason.

*I will prove it real, sir, upon the strengths
of judgment and intelligence.*

SIR TOBY BELCH
And they have been grand-jury-men since
before Noah
was a sailor.

*And they have been good members of the jury
since before Noah
built his Ark.*

FABIAN
She did show favour to the youth in your sight
only
to exasperate you, to awake your dormouse

*She only did it to make you jealous and rouse
you into action.*

valour, to
You should then have accosted her; and with some
excellent jests, fire-new from the mint, you should
have banged the youth into dumbness. This was
looked for at your hand, and this was balked: the
double gilt of this opportunity you let time wash
off, and you are now sailed into the north of my
lady's opinion; where you will hang like an icicle
on a Dutchman's beard, unless you do redeem it by
some laudable attempt either of valour or policy.

SIR TOBY BELCH
Why, then, build me thy fortunes upon the basis of
valour. Challenge me the count's youth to fight
with him; hurt him in eleven places: my niece shall
take note of it; and assure thyself, there is no
love-broker in the world can more prevail in man's
commendation with woman than report of valour.

Why, then, challenge him to a duel; that will impress her.

FABIAN
There is no way but this, Sir Andrew.

SIR ANDREW
Will either of you bear me a challenge to him?

SIR TOBY BELCH
Go, write it in a martial hand; be curst and brief;
it is no matter how witty, so it be eloquent and fun
of invention: taunt him with the licence of ink:
if thou thou'st him some thrice, it shall not be

There is no other way to do it, Sir Andrew.

Will either of you take my challenge to him?

Do it through a letter, written angrily and bravely.

amiss; and as many lies as will lie in thy sheet of
paper, although the sheet were big enough for the bed of Ware in England, set 'em down: go, about it. Let there be gall enough in thy ink, though thou write with a goose-pen, no matter: about it.

SIR ANDREW
Where shall I find you?

Where will I find you?

SIR TOBY BELCH
We'll call thee at the cubiculo: go.

We will call you at the cubiculo: go.

Exit SIR ANDREW

FABIAN
This is a dear manikin to you, Sir Toby.

That is a valuable man to you, Sir Toby.

SIR TOBY BELCH
I have been dear to him, lad, some two thousand strong, or so.

I have been valuable to him, lad, some two thousand in money, or so.

FABIAN
We shall have a rare letter from him: but you'll not deliver't?

We shall have a great letter from him: but you'll not deliver it?

SIR TOBY BELCH
Never trust me, then; and by all means stir on the
youth to an answer. I think oxen and wainropes cannot hale them together. For Andrew, if he were
opened, and you find so much blood in his liver as
will clog the foot of a flea, I'll eat the rest of the anatomy.

*I don't trust him to do well at all. You could cut him open,
and I bet you wouldn't even find enough blood to clog
the foot of a flea.*

FABIAN
And his opposite, the youth, bears in his visage no great presage of cruelty.

And the youth seems no fighter either.

SIR TOBY BELCH
Look, where the youngest wren of nine comes.

Enter MARIA

Look, where the youngest bird of nine comes.

MARIA
If you desire the spleen, and will laugh yourself into stitches, follow me. Yond gull Malvolio is turned heathen, a very renegado; for there is no Christian, that means to be saved by believing rightly, can ever believe such impossible passages
of grossness. He's in yellow stockings.

*Come see the hilarious sight! No Christian could believe
such impossible ridiculousness. He's in yellow stockings.*

SIR TOBY BELCH
And cross-gartered?

MARIA
Most villanously; like a pedant that keeps a school
i' the church. I have dogged him, like his murderer. He does obey every point of the letter that I dropped to betray him: he does smile his face into more lines than is in the new map with the
augmentation of the Indies: you have not seen such
a thing as 'tis. I can hardly forbear hurling things at him. I know my lady will strike him: if she do,
he'll smile and take't for a great favour.

And tied criss-cross?

*Hideously so. He won't stop smiling either, and I think my lady will hit him for sure, and he'll take that
as a great compliment.*

SIR TOBY BELCH
Come, bring us, bring us where he is.

Take us, take us to where he is.

Exeunt

SCENE III. A street.

Enter SEBASTIAN and ANTONIO

SEBASTIAN
I would not by my will have troubled you;
But, since you make your pleasure of your pains,
I will no further chide you.

ANTONIO
I could not stay behind you: my desire,
More sharp than filed steel, did spur me forth;
And not all love to see you, though so much
As might have drawn one to a longer voyage,
But jealousy what might befall your travel,
Being skilless in these parts; which to a stranger,
Unguided and unfriended, often prove
Rough and unhospitable: my willing love,
The rather by these arguments of fear,
Set forth in your pursuit.

[handwritten annotation: *just guys bein' dudes*]

SEBASTIAN
My kind Antonio,
I can no other answer make but thanks,
And thanks; and ever oft good turns
Are shuffled off with such uncurrent pay:
But, were my worth as is my conscience firm,
You should find better dealing. What's to do?
Shall we go see the reliques of this town?

ANTONIO
To-morrow, sir: best first go see your lodging.

SEBASTIAN
I am not weary, and 'tis long to night:
I pray you, let us satisfy our eyes
With the memorials and the things of fame
That do renown this city.

---

*I wish that I had not caused you trouble;
But since you seem to enjoy what I thought would burden you,
I will not criticize you further.*

*I could not stay behind; my wishes,
More sharp that filed steel, pushed me ahead; And not just my wanting to see you, though so much
it was enough to make me take even a longer journey,
But worry over what might happen to you in your travels, Being alone in these parts;
which to a stranger,
Without a guide or a friend, often turns out to be
Rough and without hospitality; my willing love,
Increased by these fearful thoughts, Made me run after you.*

*My dear Antonio,
I can make no other answer but thanks
And thanks; and so often such good turns
Are not repaid as they deserve to be:
But, if I were worth as much as my conscience is firm,
You should find a better reward. What should we do?
Shall we go see the sights of this town?*

Tomorrow, sir: it would be best to first find you someplace to stay.

*I'm not tired, and it is a long time before dark: Please, let us feast our eyes
With the memorials and famous things
That this city is known for.*

ANTONIO
Would you'ld pardon me;
I do not without danger walk these streets:
Once, in a sea-fight, 'gainst the count his galleys
I did some service; of such note indeed,
That were I ta'en here it would scarce be answer'd.

Forgive me, I killed a bunch of the count's men in a fight,
and if I were killed here it would not be punished.

SEBASTIAN
Belike you slew great number of his people.

So you killed a large number of his people.

ANTONIO
The offence is not of such a bloody nature;
Albeit the quality of the time and quarrel
Might well have given us bloody argument.
It might have since been answer'd in repaying
What we took from them; which, for traffic's sake,
Most of our city did: only myself stood out;
For which, if I be lapsed in this place,
I shall pay dear.

Not particularly, I am more of a scapegoat in a larger fight.

SEBASTIAN
Do not then walk too open.

Don't walk too obviously then.

ANTONIO
It doth not fit me. Hold, sir, here's my purse.
It doesn't fit me. Hold, sir, here's my wallet.
In the south suburbs, at the Elephant,
In the south part of the city, at the Elephant inn,
Is best to lodge: I will bespeak our diet,
Is the best place to stay: I will fetch out dinner,
Whiles you beguile the time and feed your knowledge

While you pass the time and feed your knowledge
With viewing of the town: there shall you have me.
With seeing the sights: there you shall meet me.

SEBASTIAN
Why I your purse?

Why give me your wallet?

ANTONIO
Haply your eye shall light upon some toy
You have desire to purchase; and your store,

It is possible you will find something you want to buy,

78

I think, is not for idle markets, sir.

SEBASTIAN
I'll be your purse-bearer and leave you
For an hour.

ANTONIO
To the Elephant.

SEBASTIAN
I do remember.

and I know you have little money.

*I'll carry your wallet and leave you
For an hour.*

To the Elephant inn.

I will remember.

Exeunt

SCENE IV. OLIVIA's garden.

Enter OLIVIA and MARIA

OLIVIA
I have sent after him: he says he'll come;
How shall I feast him? what bestow of him?
For youth is bought more oft than begg'd or borrow'd.
I speak too loud.
Where is Malvolio? he is sad and civil,
And suits well for a servant with my fortunes:
Where is Malvolio?

I have invited him here: he says he'll come; How shall I feast him? What gifts give him?
For youth is bought more often than begged or borrowed.
I speak too loudly.
Where is Malvolio? He is sad and polite, And is good for my reputation:
Where is Malvolio?

MARIA
He's coming, madam; but in very strange manner. He
is, sure, possessed, madam.

He is coming, madam; but is acting very strange. He
is surely possessed, madam.

OLIVIA
Why, what's the matter? does he rave?

Why, what's the matter? Is he ranting?

MARIA
No, madam, he does nothing but smile: your ladyship were best to have some guard about you, if
he come; for, sure, the man is tainted in's wits.

No, madam, all he does is smile: your ladyship would be safest to have some guards around you, if
he comes; for, sure, he has lost his mind.

OLIVIA
Go call him hither.

Go call him here.

Exit MARIA

I am as mad as he,
If sad and merry madness equal be.

I am as insane as he is,
If sadness and madness are equal.

Re-enter MARIA, with MALVOLIO

How now, Malvolio!

What's going on, Malvolio?

MALVOLIO
Sweet lady, ho, ho.

Sweet lady, hello, hello.

OLIVIA
Smilest thou?
I sent for thee upon a sad occasion.

MALVOLIO
Sad, lady! I could be sad: this does make some
obstruction in the blood, this cross-gartering; but
what of that? if it please the eye of one, it is
with me as the very true sonnet is, 'Please one, and
please all.'

OLIVIA
Why, how dost thou, man? what is the matter
with thee?

MALVOLIO
Not black in my mind, though yellow in my legs. It
did come to his hands, and commands shall be
executed: I think we do know the sweet Roman
hand.

OLIVIA
Wilt thou go to bed, Malvolio?

MALVOLIO
To bed! ay, sweet-heart, and I'll come to thee.

OLIVIA
God comfort thee! Why dost thou smile so and kiss
thy hand so oft?

MARIA
How do you, Malvolio?

MALVOLIO
At your request! yes; nightingales answer daws.

MARIA
Why appear you with this ridiculous boldness
before my lady?

You're smiling?
I asked for you to come on a sad occasion.

Sad, lady? I could be sad: it does make for some
loss of circulation, this cross-gartering;
but who cares? If it pleases one person, it is
with me as the very true poem says,
"Please one, and
you please all.'

Why, what is going on, man? What is the matter
with you?

My thoughts are not dark, though my legs are
yellow. It
came to his hands, and commands shall be
followed: I think we do know the sweet
handwriting.

Will you go to bed, Malvolio?

To bed! Yes, sweetheart, and I'll come to you.

God comfort you! Why do you smile like
that and kiss
your hand so often?

What are you doing, Malvolio?

At your request! yes; nightingales answer
crows.

Why are you appearing so ridiculously and
cheekily in front of my lady?

MALVOLIO
'Be not afraid of greatness:' 'twas well writ.

OLIVIA
What meanest thou by that, Malvolio?

MALVOLIO
'Some are born great,'--

OLIVIA
Ha!

MALVOLIO
'Some achieve greatness,'--

OLIVIA
What sayest thou?

MALVOLIO
'And some have greatness thrust upon them.'

OLIVIA
Heaven restore thee!

MALVOLIO
'Remember who commended thy yellow stockings,'--

OLIVIA
Thy yellow stockings!

MALVOLIO
'And wished to see thee cross-gartered.'

OLIVIA
Cross-gartered!

MALVOLIO
'Go to thou art made, if thou desirest to be so;'--

OLIVIA
Am I made?

MALVOLIO
'If not, let me see thee a servant still.'

'Do not be afraid of greatness:' it was well written.

What do you mean by that, Malvolio?

'Some are born great,'--

Ha!

'Some reach greatness,'--

What are you saying?

'And some have greatness pushed upon them.'

Heaven heal you!

'Remember who praised your yellow stockings,'

Your yellow stockings!

'And wished to see you cross-gartered.'

Cross-gartered!

'Go to you are made, if you want it to be that way;'=

Am I made what?

'If not, let me see you a servant still.'

OLIVIA
Why, this is very midsummer madness.

Servant
Madam, the young gentleman of the Count Orsino's is
returned: I could hardly entreat him back: he attends your ladyship's pleasure.

OLIVIA
I'll come to him.

Good Maria, let this fellow be looked to. Where's
my cousin Toby? Let some of my people have a special
care of him: I would not have him miscarry for the
half of my dowry.

MALVOLIO
O, ho! do you come near me now? no worse man than
Sir Toby to look to me! This concurs directly with
the letter: she sends him on purpose, that I may
appear stubborn to him; for she incites me to that
in the letter. 'Cast thy humble slough,' says she;
'be opposite with a kinsman, surly with servants;
let thy tongue tang with arguments of state; put
thyself into the trick of singularity;' and
consequently sets down the manner how; as, a sad
face, a reverend carriage, a slow tongue, in the
habit of some sir of note, and so forth. I have

Enter Servant

*Madam, the young gentleman of the Count Orsino has
returned: I could hardly tell him to go back; he wishes to please your ladyship.*

I'll go to him.

Exit Servant

*Good Maria, let this fellow be looked after. Where's
my relative Toby? Let some of my people take special
care of him: I would not have him be ill for the
half of my fortune.*

Exeunt OLIVIA and MARIA

*Oh, hey! Are you coming near me now? No worse man than
Sir Toby to look after me! This agrees directly with
the letter: she sends him to me on purpose, that I may
appear stubborn to him; for she encourages me to that
in the letter. 'Remove your humble character,' she says,
'be contrary with a kinsman, rude with the servants;*

---

limed her; but it is Jove's doing, and Jove make me
thankful! And when she went away now, 'Let this
fellow be looked to:' fellow! not Malvolio, nor
after my degree, but fellow. Why, every thing
adheres together, that no dram of a scruple, no
scruple of a scruple, no obstacle, no incredulous
or unsafe circumstance--What can be said? Nothing
that can be can come between me and the full
prospect of my hopes. Well, Jove, not I, is the
doer of this, and he is to be thanked.

and in general be outrageous, and she will love me!
What luck, and Jove is to be thanked.

Re-enter MARIA, with SIR TOBY BELCH and FABIAN

SIR TOBY BELCH
Which way is he, in the name of sanctity? If all
the devils of hell be drawn in little, and Legion
himself possessed him, yet I'll speak to him.

Where is he? Even if he's possessed by a thousand
devils from hell, I will speak to him.

FABIAN
Here he is, here he is. How is't with you, sir?
how is't with you, man?

Here he is, here he is. How is it with you, sir?
how is it with you, man?

MALVOLIO
Go off; I discard you: let me enjoy my private: go
off.

Go away, leave me alone.

MARIA
Lo, how hollow the fiend speaks within him! did not
I tell you? Sir Toby, my lady prays you to have a
care of him.

See, how evilly the devil speaks from inside him!
Did I not
tell you? Sir Toby, my lady begs you to take care of him.

MALVOLIO

Original	Modern
Ah, ha! does she so?	Ah ha! Does she now?
SIR TOBY BELCH Go to, go to; peace, peace; we must deal gently with him: let me alone. How do you, Malvolio? how is't with you? What, man! defy the devil: consider, he's an enemy to mankind.	We must be gentle with him, even if he's possessed! Fight the devil, he's an enemy to mankind.
MALVOLIO Do you know what you say?	Do you know what you're saying?
MARIA La you, an you speak ill of the devil, how he takes it at heart! Pray God, he be not bewitched!	Look, when you speak badly of the devil, he takes it personally! Please God may he not be cursed!
FABIAN Carry his water to the wise woman.	Take him to the wise woman [a kind of good doctor/witch combination of the time].
MARIA Marry, and it shall be done to-morrow morning, if I live. My lady would not lose him for more than I'll say.	By Mary, and it shall be done tomorrow morning, if I live. My lady does not want to lose him for more than I'll say.
MALVOLIO How now, mistress!	Hello, miss!
MARIA O Lord! Get him to say his prayers, good Sir Toby, get him to pray.	Oh Lord! Get him to say prayers, good Sir Toby, get him to pray.
MALVOLIO My prayers, minx!	My prayers, [insult]!
MARIA No, I warrant you, he will not hear of godliness.	No, I swear to you, he will not hear of godliness
MALVOLIO Go, hang yourselves all! you are idle shallow things: I am not of your element: you shall know more hereafter.	Go hang yourselves, all of you! You are useless, shallow things: I am not like you: you shall know more afterwards.

SIR TOBY BELCH
Is't possible?

Exit

Is it possible?

FABIAN
If this were played upon a stage now, I could condemn it as an improbable fiction.

speak badly of it as something way too unlikely.

SIR TOBY BELCH
His very genius hath taken the infection of the device, man.

His very genius has been infected by the trick, man.

MARIA
Nay, pursue him now, lest the device take air and taint.

No, run after him now, so that the trick doesn't go too far.

FABIAN
Why, we shall make him mad indeed.

Why, we shall make him actually insane.

MARIA
The house will be the quieter.

The house will be quieter if we do.

SIR TOBY BELCH
Come, we'll have him in a dark room and bound. My
niece is already in the belief that he's mad: we
may carry it thus, for our pleasure and his penance,
till our very pastime, tired out of breath, prompt
us to have mercy on him: at which time we will
bring the device to the bar and crown thee for a
finder of madmen. But see, but see.

*Come, we'll tie him up and put him in a dark room. My
niece already believes that he's insane, we
may carry it out like that, for our amusement and his punishment,
until our fun has run its course, and we decide
to have mercy on him, at which time we will
reveal the trick and honor you as a*

Enter SIR ANDREW

FABIAN
More matter for a May morning.

More fun to have on a morning in May.

SIR ANDREW
Here's the challenge, read it: warrant there's vinegar and pepper in't.

Here's the challenge, read it: I bet there's vinegar and pepper in it.

FABIAN
Is't so saucy?

Is it that saucy?

SIR ANDREW
Ay, is't, I warrant him: do but read.

Yes, it is, I do believe: just read.

SIR TOBY BELCH
Give me.

Give it to me.

Reads

'Youth, whatsoever thou art, thou art but a scurvy fellow.'

'Young man, whatever you are, you are nothing but a scurvy fellow.'

FABIAN
Good, and valiant.

Good, and brave.

SIR TOBY BELCH
[Reads] 'Wonder not, nor admire not in thy mind,
why I do call thee so, for I will show thee no reason for't.'

*'Do not be surprised, or confused in your mind,
why I call you that, for I will not show you any reason for it."*

FABIAN
A good note; that keeps you from the blow of the law.

A good point; that keeps you safe from the law.

SIR TOBY BELCH
[Reads] 'Thou comest to the lady Olivia, and in my
sight she uses thee kindly: but thou liest in thy
throat; that is not the matter I challenge thee for.'

You come to the lady Olivia, and in my sight she uses you kindly: but you lie in your throat; that is not the issue I am challenging you about.'

FABIAN
Very brief, and to exceeding good sense--less.

Very short, and very sensible.

SIR TOBY BELCH
[Reads] 'I will waylay thee going home; where if it
be thy chance to kill me,'--

'I will interrupt you going him; where if it is your fate to kill me,'--

FABIAN
Good.

Good.

SIR TOBY BELCH
[Reads] 'Thou killest me like a rogue and a villain.'

'You kill me like a rogue and a villain.'

FABIAN
Still you keep o' the windy side of the law: good.

Still you keep on the safe side of the law: good.

SIR TOBY BELCH
[Reads] 'Fare thee well; and God have mercy upon
one of our souls! He may have mercy upon mine; but
my hope is better, and so look to thyself. Thy friend, as thou usest him, and thy sworn enemy,
ANDREW AGUECHEEK. If this letter move him not, his legs cannot:
I'll give't him.

*my hope is better, and so look to yourself. You
friend, as you used him, and your sworn enemy,
If this letter does not move him, his legs cannot:
I'll give it to him.*

MARIA
You may have very fit occasion for't: he is now in
some commerce with my lady, and will by and by depart.

*You may have a good opportunity for it: he is now in
some business with my lady, and will shortly leave.*

SIR TOBY BELCH
Go, Sir Andrew: scout me for him at the corner the
orchard like a bum-baily: so soon as ever thou seest
him, draw; and, as thou drawest swear horrible; for
it comes to pass oft that a terrible oath, with a swaggering accent sharply twanged off, gives manhood
more approbation than ever proof itself would have
earned him. Away!

*Go, Sir Andrew, and as soon as you see him, draw your sword,
swearing terrible things.
Go fight!*

SIR ANDREW
Nay, let me alone for swearing.

No, let me alone for swearing.

Exit

SIR TOBY BELCH

Now will not I deliver his letter: for the behavior of the young gentleman gives him out to be of good capacity and breeding; his employment between his lord and my niece confirms no less: therefore this letter, being so excellently ignorant, will breed no terror in the youth: he will find it comes from a clodpole. But, sir, I will deliver his challenge by word of mouth; set upon Aguecheek a notable report of valour; and drive the gentleman, as I know his youth will aptly receive it, into a most hideous opinion of his rage, skill, fury and impetuosity. This will so fright them both that they will kill one another by the look, like cockatrices.

FABIAN
Here he comes with your niece: give them way till
he take leave, and presently after him.

SIR TOBY BELCH
I will meditate the while upon some horrid message
for a challenge.

OLIVIA
I have said too much unto a heart of stone
And laid mine honour too unchary out:
There's something in me that reproves my fault;
But such a headstrong potent fault it is,
That it but mocks reproof.

Now I will not deliver the letter: for the behavior skill and nobility; his employment between his lord and my niece confirms it: therefore this letter, being so incredibly stupid, will cause no terror in the young man: he will find it comes from a clod. But sir, I will deliver his challenge by word of mouth; describe the knight Aguecheek with a notable report of courage; and drive the gentleman, as I know his youth with appropriately take it, into a most terrifying opinion of his rage, skill, anger, and impatience. This will so frighten them both that they will kill [Cockatrices were half-rooster, half-snake mythological beings whose sight could turn things into stone.]

Re-enter OLIVIA, with VIOLA

Here he comes with you niece: give them room until
he leaves, and then in a moment go after him.

I will ponder for a while some horrible message
for a challenge to a duel.

Exeunt SIR TOBY BELCH, FABIAN, and MARIA

I have said too much to a heart of stone
And laid my honor not carefully enough out: There's something in my that criticizes my fault;
But it is such a strong fault,
That it only mocks being corrected.

VIOLA
With the same 'havior that your passion bears
Goes on my master's grief.

With that same behavior your passion is going on My master's grief is treating him.

OLIVIA
Here, wear this jewel for me, 'tis my picture;
Refuse it not; it hath no tongue to vex you;
And I beseech you come again to-morrow.
What shall you ask of me that I'll deny,
That honour saved may upon asking give?

Here, take this locket for me, it is my picture; Don't refuse it; it has to voice to trouble you; And I beg that you come again tomorrow. What will you ask of me that I'll refuse, That saving my honor may then give?

VIOLA
Nothing but this; your true love for my master.

Nothing but this; your true love for Duke Orsino.

OLIVIA
How with mine honour may I give him that
Which I have given to you?

How with my honor may I give him something Which I have already given you?

VIOLA
I will acquit you.

I will give you permission.

OLIVIA
Well, come again to-morrow: fare thee well:
A fiend like thee might bear my soul to hell.

Well, come again tomorrow; fare you well: A demon like you could take my soul to hell.

Exit

Re-enter SIR TOBY BELCH and FABIAN

SIR TOBY BELCH
Gentleman, God save thee.

Gentleman, God save you.

VIOLA
And you, sir.

And to you, sir.

SIR TOBY BELCH
That defence thou hast, betake thee to't: of what nature the wrongs are thou hast done him, I know
not; but thy intercepter, full of despite, bloody as the hunter, attends thee at the orchard-end: dismount thy tuck, be yare in thy preparation, for
thy assailant is quick, skilful and deadly.

Watch out, because a terrifying fighter will assault you.

VIOLA
You mistake, sir; I am sure no man hath any quarrel
to me: my remembrance is very free and clear from
any image of offence done to any man.

You are making a mistake; I am sure no man has any issue with me.

SIR TOBY BELCH
You'll find it otherwise, I assure you: therefore, if you hold your life at any price, betake you to your guard; for your opposite hath in him what youth, strength, skill and wrath can furnish man withal.

*Oh no, you are wrong, and if you value your life you should
be on your guard, for you opponent has in him what
youth, strength, skill, and anger can give a man.*

VIOLA
I pray you, sir, what is he?

SIR TOBY BELCH
He is knight, dubbed with unhatched rapier and on
carpet consideration; but he is a devil in private
brawl: souls and bodies hath he divorced three; and
his incensement at this moment is so implacable,
that satisfaction can be none but by pangs of death
and sepulchre. Hob, nob, is his word; give't or take't.

Please, sir, what is he?

*He is a knight, dubbed with a fine sword and by
royalty; but he is a devil in private brawls; he has killed three men; and
his anger at this time is so great,
that he can have no satisfaction except through
one of you dying.*

VIOLA
I will return again into the house and desire some
conduct of the lady. I am no fighter. I have heard
of some kind of men that put quarrels purposely on
others, to taste their valour: belike this is a man
of that quirk.

SIR TOBY BELCH
Sir, no; his indignation derives itself out of a

*I will go back into the house and ask some advice from the lady. I am no fighter. I have heard
of some men who deliberately pick fights with
others, to see their courage: probably this is a man
of that type.*

Sir, no; his anger takes itself out from a very

very competent injury: therefore, get you on and give him his desire. Back you shall not to the
house, unless you undertake that with me which with
as much safety you might answer him: therefore, on,
or strip your sword stark naked; for meddle you
must, that's certain, or forswear to wear iron about you.

*real offense: therefore, go on and
give him what he wants. You should not go back into
the house, unless you fight with me instead
therefore, go on to meet him,
or unsheath your sword; for fight you must,
or swear to wear a weapon at all times.*

VIOLA
This is as uncivil as strange. I beseech you, do me
this courteous office, as to know of the knight what
my offence to him is: it is something of my
negligence, nothing of my purpose.

*This is as barbaric as strange. I beg you, do me
this polite favor, as to find out from the night what
my offense to him is: it is something of my mistake, nothing I have done on purpose.*

SIR TOBY BELCH
I will do so. Signior Fabian, stay you by this gentleman till my return.

I will do that. Sir Fabian, stay by this gentleman until I return.

Exit

VIOLA
Pray you, sir, do you know of this matter?

Please, sir, do you know of this matter?

FABIAN
I know the knight is incensed against you, even to a
mortal arbitrement; but nothing of the circumstance more.

*I know the knight is angry against you, even to a
duel to the death; but nothing more.*

VIOLA
I beseech you, what manner of man is he?

Please, what kind of man is he?

FABIAN
Nothing of that wonderful promise, to read him by
his form, as you are like to find him in the proof of his valour. He is, indeed, sir, the most

One of the best fighters and fearsome men in Illyria.

skilful,
bloody and fatal opposite that you could possibly
have found in any part of Illyria. Will you walk
towards him? I will make your peace with him if I
can.

VIOLA
I shall be much bound to you for't: I am one that
had rather go with sir priest than sir knight: I
care not who knows so much of my mettle.

I would be very distressed about it: I am one that would rather go with sir priest than sir knight: I do not care who knows that about my courage.

Exeunt

Re-enter SIR TOBY BELCH, with SIR ANDREW

SIR TOBY BELCH
[To VIOLA] There's no remedy, sir; he will fight
with you for's oath sake: marry, he hath better
bethought him of his quarrel, and he finds that now
scarce to be worth talking of: therefore draw, for
the supportance of his vow; he protests he will not hurt you.

There's no solution, sir; he will fight with you for the sake of this oath: by Mary, he has thought better of the quarrel, and he finds that now it is not worth talking of: therefore draw, for the sake of his promise; he protests he will not hurt you.

VIOLA
[Aside] Pray God defend me! A little thing would
make me tell them how much I lack of a man.

[Aside] May God defend me! A little thing would make me tell them how little of a man I am.

FABIAN
Give ground, if you see him furious.

Give him ground, if you see him angry.

SIR TOBY BELCH
Come, Sir Andrew, there's no remedy; the gentleman
will, for his honour's sake, have one bout with you;
he cannot by the duello avoid it: but he has
promised me, as he is a gentleman and a

Come, Sir Andrew, there's no solution; the gentleman will, for his honor's sake, have one match with you; he cannot by the warrior code avoid it: but he has promised me, as he is a soldier, he will not hurt you. Come on; to't.

SIR ANDREW
Pray God, he keep his oath!

VIOLA
I do assure you, 'tis against my will.

ANTONIO
Put up your sword. If this young gentleman
Have done offence, I take the fault on me:
If you offend him, I for him defy you.

SIR TOBY BELCH
You, sir! why, what are you?

ANTONIO
One, sir, that for his love dares yet do more
Than you have heard him brag to you he will.

SIR TOBY BELCH
Nay, if you be an undertaker, I am for you.

FABIAN
O good Sir Toby, hold! here come the officers.

SIR TOBY BELCH
I'll be with you anon.

VIOLA
Pray, sir, put your sword up, if you please.

First Officer
This is the man; do thy office.

Second Officer
Antonio, I arrest thee at the suit of Count Orsino.

ANTONIO

---

nobleman and a soldier, he will not hurt you. Come on; start.

Pray God, he keeps his promise!

They draw

Enter ANTONIO

Put away your sword. If this young nobleman Has done offense, I take it as my fault: If you offend him, I defy you for him.

You, sir! Why, who are you?

One, sir, that for his love dares to do still more Than you have heard him brag to you that he will.

No, if you are taking this on, I will for you. They draw

Enter Officers

Oh, good Sir Toby, stop! Here come the police.

I'll be with you in a moment.

Please, sir, put your sword away, please.

This is the man; do you job.

Antonio, I arrest you for the sake of Count Orsino.

You do mistake me, sir. | *You are making a mistake, sir.*

First Officer
No, sir, no jot; I know your favour well, | *No sir, not one bit; I know you well.*
Though now you have no sea-cap on your head | *Though you do not have your former hat on your head*
Take him away: he knows I know him well. | *Take him away: he knows that I know him well.*

ANTONIO
I must obey. | *I must do what they say.*
| *To VIOLA*
This comes with seeking you: | *This comes from looking for you:*
But there's no remedy; I shall answer it. | *But there's no solution; I must answer it.*
What will you do, now my necessity | *What will you do, now that my troubles*
Makes me to ask you for my purse? It grieves me | *Makes me ask you for my wallet? It causes me pain*
Much more for what I cannot do for you | *Much more for what I cannot do for you*
Than what befalls myself. You stand amazed; | *Than what happens to me myself. You stand amazed;*
But be of comfort. | *But be comforted.*

Second Officer
Come, sir, away. | *Come on, sir, let's go.*

ANTONIO
I must beg you some of that money. | *I must beg from you some of that money.*

VIOLA
What money, sir? | *What money, sir?*
For the fair kindness you have show'd me here, | *For the great kindness you have shown me here,*
And, part, being prompted by your present trouble, | *And, partly, as prompted by your current troubles,*
Out of my lean and low ability | *Out of my limited amount of money*
I'll lend you something: my having is not much; | *I'll lend you something: I do not have much;*
I'll make division of my present with you: | *I'll give part of what I have at the moment with you:*
Hold, there's half my coffer. | *Hold, here's half my wallet.*

ANTONIO
Will you deny me now? | *What? You're being ungrateful.*
Is't possible that my deserts to you
Can lack persuasion? Do not tempt my misery,
Lest that it make me so unsound a man
As to upbraid you with those kindnesses
That I have done for you.

VIOLA
I know of none;
Nor know I you by voice or any feature:
I hate ingratitude more in a man
Than lying, vainness, babbling, drunkenness,
Or any taint of vice whose strong corruption
Inhabits our frail blood.

What?? You are the one being ungrateful!

ANTONIO
O heavens themselves!

Oh by heaven!

Second Officer
Come, sir, I pray you, go.

Come on sir, please, go.

ANTONIO
Let me speak a little. This youth that you see here
I snatch'd one half out of the jaws of death,
Relieved him with such sanctity of love,
And to his image, which methought did promise
Most venerable worth, did I devotion.

But I saved his life!

ANTONIO
But O how vile an idol proves this god
Thou hast, Sebastian, done good feature shame.
In nature there's no blemish but the mind;
None can be call'd deform'd but the unkind:
Virtue is beauty, but the beauteous evil
Are empty trunks o'erflourish'd by the devil.

Oh, Sebastian, I am very disappointed in you.

First Officer
The man grows mad: away with him! Come, come, sir.

ANTONIO
Lead me on.

This man is going crazy: away with him! Come on, sir.

Take me away.

VIOLA
Methinks his words do from such passion fly,
That he believes himself: so do not I.
Prove true, imagination, O, prove true,
That I, dear brother, be now ta'en for you!

Exit with Officers

Oh, he mistook me for Sebastian! Please, may I be right!

96

SIR TOBY BELCH
Come hither, knight; come hither, Fabian: we'll whisper o'er a couplet or two of most sage saws.

Come here, knight; come here, Fabian: we'll whisper a few poems and stories that we know.

VIOLA
He named Sebastian: I my brother know
Yet living in my glass; even such and so
In favour was my brother, and he went
Still in this fashion, colour, ornament,
For him I imitate: O, if it prove,
Tempests are kind and salt waves fresh in love.

*I deliberately copied Sebastian, so I am mistaken for him,
May it turn out that the storms are kind and salt waves fresh in love.*

Exit

SIR TOBY BELCH
A very dishonest paltry boy, and more a coward than
a hare: his dishonesty appears in leaving his
friend here in necessity and denying him; and for
his cowardship, ask Fabian.

*A very dishonest worthless boy, and more a coward than
a rabbit is: his dishonesty appears in leaving his
friend when he needed him and denying him; and for
his cowardliness, ask Fabian.*

FABIAN
A coward, a most devout coward, religious in it.

A coward, a terrible coward like it was his religion.

SIR ANDREW
'Slid, I'll after him again and beat him.

I'll run after him again and beat him.

SIR TOBY BELCH
Do; cuff him soundly, but never draw thy sword.

Do; hit him soundly, but never draw your sword.

SIR ANDREW
An I do not,--

If I do not,--

FABIAN
Come, let's see the event.

Let's go see this happen.

SIR TOBY BELCH
I dare lay any money 'twill be nothing yet.

I'd be willing to bet money it doesn't happen.

Exeunt

ACT IV

SCENE I. Before OLIVIA's house.

Enter SEBASTIAN and Clown

Clown
Will you make me believe that I am not sent for you?

Will you make me believe that I am not sent to fetch you?

SEBASTIAN
Go to, go to, thou art a foolish fellow:
Let me be clear of thee.

*Enough, enough, you are a foolish fellow:
Get away from me.*

Clown
Well held out, i' faith! No, I do not know you; nor
I am not sent to you by my lady, to bid you come
speak with her; nor your name is not Master Cesario;
nor this is not my nose neither. Nothing that is so is so.

*Well held out, by my faith! No, I do not know you; and
I am not sent to you by my lady, to tell you to come
speak with her, and your name is not Master Cesario;
and this is not my nose either. Nothing that is, is.*

SEBASTIAN
I prithee, vent thy folly somewhere else:
Thou know'st not me.

I beg you, spend your foolishness somewhere else: You do not know me.

Enter SIR ANDREW, SIR TOBY BELCH, and FABIAN

SIR ANDREW
Now, sir, have I met you again? there's for you.

Now, sir, have I meet you again? There you are.

SEBASTIAN
Why, there's for thee, and there, and there. Are all
the people mad?

*Why there's for you, and there, and there. Are all
the people insane?*

SIR TOBY BELCH
Hold, sir, or I'll throw your dagger o'er the house.

Stop, sir, or I'll throw your dagger over the house.

Clown
This will I tell my lady straight: I would not be in some of your coats for two pence.

I sure wouldn't want to be in your shoes.

Exit

SIR TOBY BELCH
Come on, sir; hold.

Come, sir; fight.

SIR ANDREW
Nay, let him alone: I'll go another way to work with him; I'll have an action of battery against
him, if there be any law in Illyria: though I struck him first, yet it's no matter for that.

*No, leave him alone: I'll go another way to work with him; I'll charge him with assault
if there is any law in Illyria: though I hit him first, yet it's not important.*

SEBASTIAN
Let go thy hand.

Get your hand off me.

SIR TOBY BELCH
Come, sir, I will not let you go. Come, my young
soldier, put up your iron: you are well fleshed; come on.

*Come, sir, I will not let you go. Come on, my young
soldier, draw your sword: you are fit enough; come on.*

SEBASTIAN
I will be free from thee. What wouldst thou now? If
thou darest tempt me further, draw thy sword.

*I want to get rid of you. What do you want now? If
you dare tempt me further, draw your sword.*

SIR TOBY BELCH
What, what? Nay, then I must have an ounce or two
of this malapert blood from you.

*What, what? No, then I must have an ounce or two
of this bad blood from you.*

Enter OLIVIA

OLIVIA
Hold, Toby; on thy life I charge thee, hold!

Stop, Toby; on your life I command you, hold!

SIR TOBY BELCH
Madam!

My lady!

OLIVIA
Will it be ever thus? Ungracious wretch,
Fit for the mountains and the barbarous caves,
Where manners ne'er were preach'd! out of my sight!
Be not offended, dear Cesario.
Rudesby, be gone!

*Will it always be like this? [Insult]
Suitable only to live out in the mountains and caves
Where there is no such thing as manners! Out of my sight!
Do not be offended, dear Cesario.
[Insult] be gone!*

Exeunt SIR TOBY BELCH, SIR ANDREW, and FABIAN

I prithee, gentle friend,	*Please, gentle friend,*
Let thy fair wisdom, not thy passion, sway	*Let your lovely wisdom, not your anger, rule*
In this uncivil and thou unjust extent	*In this impolite and extremely unfair extent*
Against thy peace. Go with me to my house,	*Against your peace. Go with me to my house,*
And hear thou there how many fruitless pranks	*And hear from me there how many unsuccessful pranks*
This ruffian hath botch'd up, that thou thereby	*This ruffian has messed up, and that you therefore*
Mayst smile at this: thou shalt not choose but go:	*May smile at this: you shall not choose to do anything else:*
Do not deny. Beshrew his soul for me,	*Do not deny it. Forgive his soul for me,*
He started one poor heart of mine in thee.	*He started one poor heart of mine in you.*

SEBASTIAN

What relish is in this? how runs the stream? / Or I am mad, or else this is a dream: / Let fancy still my sense in Lethe steep; / If it be thus to dream, still let me sleep!

What delight is this? How is this happening? Or I am insane, or else this is a dream: Let I still stay in the waters of forgetfulness; If this is what dreaming is like, let me still sleep!

OLIVIA

Nay, come, I prithee; would thou'ldst be ruled by me!

No, come, please; I wish you would do as I say!

SEBASTIAN

Madam, I will.

My lady, I will.

OLIVIA

O, say so, and so be!

Oh, say so, and may it be so!

Exeunt

SCENE II. OLIVIA's house.

Enter MARIA and Clown

MARIA
Nay, I prithee, put on this gown and this beard;
make him believe thou art Sir Topas the curate: do
it quickly; I'll call Sir Toby the whilst.

No, please, put on these robes and this beard; make him believe you are Sir Topas the minister: do it quickly; I'll call Sir Toby while you do.

Exit

Clown
Well, I'll put it on, and I will dissemble myself
in't; and I would I were the first that ever
dissembled in such a gown. I am not tall enough to
become the function well, nor lean enough to be
thought a good student; but to be said an honest man
and a good housekeeper goes as fairly as to say a
careful man and a great scholar. The competitors enter.

Well, I'll put it on, and I will be untrue to myself in it; and I wish that I were the first that ever deceived others in such robes. I am not tall enough to resemble the function well, nor lean enough to be thought a good student; but to be called an honest man and a good housekeeper is as good as to say a careful man and a great scholar. The players enter.

Enter SIR TOBY BELCH and MARIA

SIR TOBY BELCH
Jove bless thee, master Parson.

Jove bless you, master Priest.

MALVOLIO
[Within] Who calls there?

[Inside] Who's there?

Clown
Sir Topas the curate, who comes to visit Malvolio
the lunatic.

Sir Topas the minister, who comes to visit Malvolio the insane man.

MALVOLIO
Sir Topas, Sir Topas, good Sir Topas, go to my lady.

Sir Topas, Sir Topas, good Sir Topas, go to my lady.

Clown
Out, hyperbolical fiend! how vexest thou this man!
talkest thou nothing but of ladies?

Out, terrible devil! How you trouble this man! Do you talk of nothing but ladies!

SIR TOBY BELCH Well said, Master Parson.	*Well said, Priest.*
MALVOLIO Sir Topas, never was man thus wronged: good Sir Topas, do not think I am mad: they have laid me here in hideous darkness.	*Sir Topas, no man has ever been so wronged; good Sir Topas, do not think I am insane: they have placed me here in terrible darkness.*
Clown Fie, thou dishonest Satan! I call thee by the most modest terms; for I am one of those gentle ones that will use the devil himself with courtesy: sayest thou that house is dark?	*Out, you dishonest Satan! I call you by the most moderate terms; for I am one of the gentle ones that will treat the devil himself with courtesy: are you saying that house is dark?*
MALVOLIO As hell, Sir Topas.	*As hell is, Sir Topas.*
Clown Why it hath bay windows transparent as barricadoes, and the clearstores toward the south north are as lustrous as ebony; and yet complainest thou of obstruction?	*Why, it's beautiful and bright, and yet you say it is dark?*
MALVOLIO I am not mad, Sir Topas: I say to you, this house is dark.	
Clown Madman, thou errest: I say, there is no darkness but ignorance; in which thou art more puzzled than the Egyptians in their fog.	*Madman, you are wrong: I say, there is no darkness but ignorance; in which you are more puzzled than the Egyptians were in their ignorance.*
MALVOLIO I say, this house is as dark as ignorance, though ignorance were as dark as hell; and I say, there was never man thus abused. I am no more mad than you are: make the trial of it in any constant question.	*I say, this house is as dark as ignorance, even if ignorance was as dark as hell; and I say, there was never a man treated so badly. I am no more mad than you ask me a question, any question to prove it.*

Clown
What is the opinion of Pythagoras concerning wild fowl?

What is the opinion of Pythagoras about wild birds?

MALVOLIO
That the soul of our grandam might haply inhabit a bird.

That it is possible for the soul of our grandfather to be inside a bird.

Clown
What thinkest thou of his opinion?

What do you think of his opinion?

MALVOLIO
I think nobly of the soul, and no way approve his opinion.

I think well of the soul, and do not approve of his opinion.

Clown
Fare thee well. Remain thou still in darkness:
thou shalt hold the opinion of Pythagoras ere I will
allow of thy wits, and fear to kill a woodcock, lest
thou dispossess the soul of thy grandam. Fare thee well.

*Farewell. Stay still in darkness:
you shall hold the opinion of Pythagoras before I will
think you are sane, and be afraid to kill a bird, in case
you destroy the soul of your grandfather. Farewell.*

MALVOLIO
Sir Topas, Sir Topas!

Sir Topas, Sir Topas!

SIR TOBY BELCH
My most exquisite Sir Topas!

My most wonderful Sir Topas!

MARIA
Thou mightst have done this without thy beard and
gown: he sees thee not.

*You might have done this without your beard and
robes: he does not see you.*

SIR TOBY BELCH
To him in thine own voice, and bring me word how
thou findest him: I would we were well rid of this
knavery. If he may be conveniently delivered, I
would he were, for I am now so far in offence with
my niece that I cannot pursue with any

*Go to him in your own voice, and tell me how
you find him: I would rather we were finished with this
trickery. If he may be conveniently rescued, I would
like him to be, for I am now so far in offense with
my niece that I cannot safely continue with*

safety this sport to the upshot. Come by and by to my chamber.	*this prank. Come soon to my room.*
	Exeunt SIR TOBY BELCH and MARIA
Clown [Singing]'Hey, Robin, jolly Robin, Tell me how thy lady does.'	*'Hey Robin, jolly Robin, Tell me how your lady is.'*
MALVOLIO Fool!	*Clown!*
Clown 'My lady is unkind, perdy.'	*'My lady is unkind, birdie.'*
MALVOLIO Fool!	*Clown!*
Clown 'Alas, why is she so?'	*'Oh dear, why is she that way?'*
MALVOLIO Fool, I say!	*Hey, Clown!*
Clown 'She loves another'--Who calls, ha?	*'She loves someone else' - Who's calling me?*
MALVOLIO Good fool, as ever thou wilt deserve well at my hand, help me to a candle, and pen, ink and paper: as I am a gentleman, I will live to be thankful to thee for't.	*Good fool, as ever you will deserve good things from me, help me to a candle, and pen, ink, and paper, as I am a nobleman, I will live to be thankful to you for it.*
Clown Master Malvolio?	*Mister Malvolio?*
MALVOLIO Ay, good fool.	*Yes, good fool.*
Clown Alas, sir, how fell you besides your five wits?	*Oh dear, sir, how did you lose your five senses?*
MALVOLIO Fool, there was never a man so notoriously	*Fool, there was never a man so terribly*

abused: I
am as well in my wits, fool, as thou art.

Clown
But as well? then you are mad indeed, if you be no
better in your wits than a fool.

MALVOLIO
They have here propertied me; keep me in darkness,
send ministers to me, asses, and do all they can to
face me out of my wits.

Clown
Alas, sir, be patient. What say you sir? I am
sent for speaking to you.

MALVOLIO
Good fool, help me to some light and some paper: I
tell thee, I am as well in my wits as any man in Illyria.

Clown
Well-a-day that you were, sir

MALVOLIO
By this hand, I am. Good fool, some ink, paper and
light; and convey what I will set down to my lady:
it shall advantage thee more than ever the bearing
of letter did.

Clown
I will help you to't. But tell me true, are you
not mad indeed? or do you but counterfeit?

MALVOLIO
Believe me, I am not; I tell thee true.

---

treated: I
am as well in my senses, fool, as you are.

But as well? Then you must be crazy, if you are no
better in your intelligence than a fool.

They have here imprisoned me; keep me in darkness,
trick me out of my senses.

Well, sir, be patient. What do you have to say? I
have been asked to speak to you.

Good fool, please get me some light and some paper: I
tell you, I am as well as any man in Illyria.

I hope you are, sir.

By my hand, I am. Good fool, bring me some ink, paper, and
and take what I write down to my lady:
it shall be of more advantage to you than any other carrying
of a letter ever did.

I will help you to it. But tell me truly, are you
sane indeed? Or are you just faking?

Believe me, I am not; I tell you truly.

Clown
Nay, I'll ne'er believe a madman till I see his brains. I will fetch you light and paper and ink.

MALVOLIO
Fool, I'll requite it in the highest degree: I prithee, be gone.

Clown
[Singing] I am gone, sir,
And anon, sir,
I'll be with you again,
In a trice
Like to the old Vice,
Your need to sustain;
Who, with dagger of lath,
In his rage and his wrath,
Cries, ah, ha! to the devil:
Like a mad lad,
Pare thy nails, dad;
Adieu, good man devil.

No, I will never believe a madman until I see his brains. I will go get you a light and paper and ink.

Fool, I'll repay it in the greatest amount: I beg you, go.

*I am leaving, sir
And soon, sir,
I'll be back with you again,
In a moment,
Like sin,
You need to keep going,
Who, with a weapon
In his anger,
Yells at the devil:
Like a crazy man,
Trim your nails, man;
Farewell, good man devil.*

Exit

SCENE III. OLIVIA's garden.

Enter SEBASTIAN

SEBASTIAN
This is the air; that is the glorious sun;
This pearl she gave me, I do feel't and see't;
And though 'tis wonder that enwraps me thus,
Yet 'tis not madness. Where's Antonio, then?
I could not find him at the Elephant:
Yet there he was; and there I found this credit,
That he did range the town to seek me out.
His counsel now might do me golden service;
For though my soul disputes well with my sense,
That this may be some error, but no madness,
Yet doth this accident and flood of fortune
So far exceed all instance, all discourse,
That I am ready to distrust mine eyes
And wrangle with my reason that persuades me
To any other trust but that I am mad
Or else the lady's mad; yet, if 'twere so,
She could not sway her house, command her followers,
Take and give back affairs and their dispatch
With such a smooth, discreet and stable bearing
As I perceive she does: there's something in't
That is deceiveable. But here the lady comes.

This is the air; that is the beautiful sun;
This pearl she gave me, I do feel it and see it:
And though it is amazement that wraps around me,
Yet it is not madness. Where's Antonio, then?
I could not find him at the Elephant Inn:
Yet there he was at some point; and there I found out
That he wandered all around the city to look for me.
His advice might now do me some service;
For though my soul argues with my senses,
That this may be some mistake, but not insanity,
Yet this strange turn of fate
Is so far beyond anything I've ever heard of That
I am ready to distrust my own eyes
And wrestle with my reason that persuades me
To any other conclusion but that I am insane
Or else the lady's mad, yet if it were that way,
She could not rule her house, command her followers,
Take and give back business and carrying things out
In such a capable and noble fashion
As I see she does: there's something in it
That could involve trickery. But here the lady comes.

Enter OLIVIA and Priest

OLIVIA
Blame not this haste of mine. If you mean well,
Now go with me and with this holy man
Into the chantry by: there, before him,
And underneath that consecrated roof,

Do not blame me for rushing things. If you mean well, Now go with me and with this priest
Into the church: there, in front of him,
And underneath that roof that has been made

Plight me the full assurance of your faith;
That my most jealous and too doubtful soul
May live at peace. He shall conceal it
Whiles you are willing it shall come to note,
What time we will our celebration keep
According to my birth. What do you say?

SEBASTIAN
I'll follow this good man, and go with you;
And, having sworn truth, ever will be true.

OLIVIA
Then lead the way, good father; and heavens so shine,
That they may fairly note this act of mine!

sacred,
Marry me, and we will celebrate. What do you say?

I'll follow this priest, and go with you;
And having promised to be loyal, will always be loyal.

Then lead the way, good Father, and may the heavens so shine,
That they may beautifully observe this thing I am doing!

Exeunt

ACT V

SCENE I. Before OLIVIA's house.

Enter Clown and FABIAN

FABIAN
Now, as thou lovest me, let me see his letter.

Now, as you love me, let me see his letter

Clown
Good Master Fabian, grant me another request.

Good Mister Fabian, do another thing for me.

FABIAN
Any thing.

Anything.

Clown
Do not desire to see this letter.

Do not ask to see this letter.

FABIAN
This is, to give a dog, and in recompense desire my dog again.

This is, to give a dog, and in return ask for my dog again.

Enter DUKE ORSINO, VIOLA, CURIO, and Lords

DUKE ORSINO
Belong you to the Lady Olivia, friends?

Do you belong to the Lady Olivia, friends?

Clown
Ay, sir; we are some of her trappings.

Yes, sir, we are some of her belongings.

DUKE ORSINO
I know thee well; how dost thou, my good fellow?

I know you well; how are you, my good fellow?

Clown
Truly, sir, the better for my foes and the worse for my friends.

Truly, sir, improved by my enemies and worsened by my friends.

DUKE ORSINO
Just the contrary; the better for thy friends.

Oh no, it's the other way around; improved by your friends.

Clown
No, sir, the worse.

No, sir, made worse.

DUKE ORSINO
How can that be?

How is that possible?

Clown
Marry, sir, they praise me and make an ass of me;
now my foes tell me plainly I am an ass: so that by
my foes, sir I profit in the knowledge of myself,
and by my friends, I am abused: so that,
conclusions to be as kisses, if your four negatives
make your two affirmatives why then, the worse for
my friends and the better for my foes.

DUKE ORSINO
Why, this is excellent.

Clown
By my troth, sir, no; though it please you to be
one of my friends.

DUKE ORSINO
Thou shalt not be the worse for me: there's gold.

Clown
But that it would be double-dealing, sir, I would
you could make it another.

DUKE ORSINO
O, you give me ill counsel.

Clown
Put your grace in your pocket, sir, for this once,
and let your flesh and blood obey it.

DUKE ORSINO
Well, I will be so much a sinner, to be a
double-dealer: there's another.

Clown
Primo, secundo, tertio, is a good play; and the old
saying is, the third pays for all: the triplex,
sir, is a good tripping measure; or the bells of
Saint Bennet, sir, may put you in mind; one,

By Mary, sir, they praise me and make an ass of me;
now my enemies tell me plainly that I am an ass; so that by
my enemies, sir, I gain knowledge about myself,
and by my friends, sir, I am lied to: so that, conclusions being kisses, if your four noes
make two yeses, why then, the worse for my friends and the better for me foes.

Very clever.

By the truth, sir, no; though it pleases you to be one of my friends.

You shall not be the worse for me: here's some money.

Except for it being double-dealing, sir, i wish you could give me more.

Oh, you give me bad advice.

Put your wisdom in your pocket, sir, this once, and let your body obey it.

Well, I will sin this much: to be a double-dealer: there's another coin.

One, two, three, is a good sequence; and the old saying is, the third pays for all: the triple, sir, is a good unit; or the bells of Saint Bennet's cathedral, sir, will make you think; one, two, three.

two, three.

DUKE ORSINO
You can fool no more money out of me at this throw:
if you will let your lady know I am here to speak
with her, and bring her along with you, it may awake
my bounty further.

You can trick no more money out of me at this time:
If you will let your lady know I am hear to speak
with her, and bring her with you, it may cause me to share
my wealth further.

Clown
Marry, sir, lullaby to your bounty till I come again. I go, sir; but I would not have you to think
but, as you say, sir, let your bounty take a nap, I
will awake it anon.

By Mary, sir, may your money sleep until I come that my desire of having is the sin of covetousness:
I will awaken it shortly.

Exit

VIOLA
Here comes the man, sir, that did rescue me.

Here comes the man, sir, that rescued me.

Enter ANTONIO and Officers

DUKE ORSINO
That face of his I do remember well;
As black as Vulcan in the smoke of war:
A bawbling vessel was he captain of,
For shallow draught and bulk unprizable;
With which such scathful grapple did he make
With the most noble bottom of our fleet,
That very envy and the tongue of loss
Cried fame and honour on him. What's the matter?

Yet, when I saw it last, it was besmear'd
I remember his face, but much dirtier and bloodier, in wartime.

First Officer
Orsino, this is that Antonio
That took the Phoenix and her fraught from Candy;
And this is he that did the Tiger board,
When your young nephew Titus lost his leg:
In private brabble did we apprehend him.

Orsino, this is that Antonio
That took the Phoenix and her freight from Candy;
And it is him that boarded the Tiger,
Where your young nephew Titus lost his leg:
We arrested him in a private fight.

VIOLA
He did me kindness, sir, drew on my side;
But in conclusion put strange speech upon

He was kind to me, sir, tried to fight on my side, But in concluding it said strange

me:
I know not what 'twas but distraction.

DUKE ORSINO
Notable pirate! thou salt-water thief!
What foolish boldness brought thee to their mercies,
Whom thou, in terms so bloody and so dear,
Hast made thine enemies?

ANTONIO
Orsino, noble sir,
Be pleased that I shake off these names you give me:
Antonio never yet was thief or pirate,
Though I confess, on base and ground enough,
Orsino's enemy. A witchcraft drew me hither:
That most ingrateful boy there by your side,
From the rude sea's enraged and foamy mouth
Did I redeem; a wreck past hope he was:
His life I gave him and did thereto add
My love, without retention or restraint,
All his in dedication; for his sake
Did I expose myself, pure for his love,
Into the danger of this adverse town;
Drew to defend him when he was beset:
Where being apprehended, his false cunning,
Not meaning to partake with me in danger,
Taught him to face me out of his acquaintance,
And grew a twenty years removed thing
While one would wink; denied me mine own purse,
Which I had recommended to his use
Not half an hour before.

VIOLA
How can this be?

DUKE ORSINO
When came he to this town?

ANTONIO
To-day, my lord; and for three months before,
No interim, not a minute's vacancy,

things to me:
That I did not understand, except as a distraction.

What made you do something so risky as that?

I saved his life, and then he repaid my by denying me, and
not giving back the money I had given him less than half an hour before.

How can this be possible?

When did he come to this town?

Today, my lord, and for three months before then, Without a pause, without even a minute

114

Both day and night did we keep company.

apart For every day and night we stayed together.

Enter OLIVIA and Attendants

DUKE ORSINO
Here comes the countess: now heaven walks on earth.
But for thee, fellow; fellow, thy words are madness:
Three months this youth hath tended upon me;
But more of that anon. Take him aside.

*But as for you, fellow; fellow, your words are insanity:
This youth has served me for three months;
But more of that in a moment. Take him aside.*

OLIVIA
What would my lord, but that he may not have,
Wherein Olivia may seem serviceable?
Cesario, you do not keep promise with me.

*What does my lord want, but that he may not have, Where Olivia may seem enough?
Cesario, you do not keep your promise to me.*

VIOLA
Madam!

My lady!

DUKE ORSINO
Gracious Olivia,--

Dear Olivia,-

OLIVIA
What do you say, Cesario? Good my lord,--

What do you say, Cesario? My good sir,--

VIOLA
My lord would speak; my duty hushes me.

My lord wishes to speak; my duty means I must be quiet.

DUKE ORSINO
Still so cruel?

Still so cruel?

OLIVIA
Still so constant, lord.

Still so loyal, Lord.

DUKE ORSINO
What, to perverseness? you uncivil lady,
To whose ingrate and unauspicious altars
My soul the faithfull'st offerings hath breathed out
That e'er devotion tender'd! What shall I do?

*What, to contrariness? You rude lady,
To whose ungrateful and unlucky altars
My soul has given the most faithful offerings
That devotion ever gave? What shall I do.*

OLIVIA
Where goes Cesario?

Where is Cesario going?

VIOLA
After him I love
More than I love these eyes, more than my life,
More, by all mores, than e'er I shall love wife.
If I do feign, you witnesses above
Punish my life for tainting of my love!

After him that I love
More than I love my eyes, more than my life,
More, by all the more, than I ever shall love a
wife. If I lie, may Heaven's witnesses Punish my
life for spoiling my love!

OLIVIA
Ay me, detested! how am I beguiled!

Oh, me, hated! How I am tricked!

VIOLA
Who does beguile you? who does do you wrong?

Who tricks you? Who does you wrong?

OLIVIA
Hast thou forgot thyself? is it so long?

Have you forgotten yourself? Is it so long?

Call forth the holy father.

DUKE ORSINO
Come, away!

OLIVIA
Whither, my lord? Cesario, husband, stay.

Where, my lord? Cesario, husband, stay.

DUKE ORSINO
Husband!

OLIVIA
Ay, husband: can he that deny?

Yes, husband: can he deny that?

DUKE ORSINO
Her husband, sirrah!

Her husband, sir!

VIOLA
No, my lord, not I.

No, my lord, not me.

OLIVIA
Alas, it is the baseness of thy fear
That makes thee strangle thy propriety:
Fear not, Cesario; take thy fortunes up;
Be that thou know'st thou art, and then thou art
As great as that thou fear'st.

Don't be afraid, Cesario, we're safe.

Enter Priest

O, welcome, father!
Father, I charge thee, by thy reverence,
Here to unfold, though lately we intended
To keep in darkness what occasion now
Reveals before 'tis ripe, what thou dost know
Hath newly pass'd between this youth and me.

Priest, tell them what we just did.

Priest
A contract of eternal bond of love,
Confirm'd by mutual joinder of your hands,
Attested by the holy close of lips,
Strengthen'd by interchangement of your rings;
And all the ceremony of this compact
Seal'd in my function, by my testimony:
Since when, my watch hath told me, toward my grave
I have travell'd but two hours.

Less than two hours ago, I married these two.

DUKE ORSINO
O thou dissembling cub! what wilt thou be
When time hath sow'd a grizzle on thy case?
Or will not else thy craft so quickly grow,
That thine own trip shall be thine overthrow?
Farewell, and take her; but direct thy feet
Where thou and I henceforth may never meet.

*You liar and traitor! Fine then, marry her, take her,
but I never want to see you again.*

VIOLA
My lord, I do protest--

OLIVIA
O, do not swear!
Hold little faith, though thou hast too much fear.

My lord, I protest--

Oh, do not swear! Have a little faith, even if you have too much fear.

SIR ANDREW
For the love of God, a surgeon! Send one presently
to Sir Toby.

Enter SIR ANDREW

For the love of God, a doctor! Send one soon to Sir Toby.

OLIVIA
What's the matter?

What's going on?

SIR ANDREW
He has broke my head across and has given Sir Toby
a bloody coxcomb too: for the love of God, your help! I had rather than forty pound I were at home.

He has punched me and given Sir Toby a bloody wound!
I wish I were at home.

OLIVIA
Who has done this, Sir Andrew?

Who has done this, Sir Andrew?

SIR ANDREW
The count's gentleman, one Cesario: we took him for
a coward, but he's the very devil incardinate.

The count's nobleman, Cesario: we thought he was
a coward, but he's the very devil himself.

DUKE ORSINO
My gentleman, Cesario?

My servant, Cesario?

SIR ANDREW
'Od's lifelings, here he is! You broke my head for
nothing; and that that I did, I was set on to do't
by Sir Toby.

By God, here he is! You broke my head for nothing; and what I did, I was put up to by Sir Toby.

VIOLA
Why do you speak to me? I never hurt you:
You drew your sword upon me without cause;
But I bespoke you fair, and hurt you not.

Why do you speak to me like this? I never hurt you: You pulled out your sword at me without a reason; But I spoke well to you, and did not hurt you.

Enter SIR TOBY BELCH and Clown

DUKE ORSINO
How now, gentleman! how is't with you?

Hello, gentleman! How are you?

SIR TOBY BELCH
That's all one: he has hurt me, and there's the end
on't. Sot, didst see Dick surgeon, sot?

That's not important: he has hurt me, and that's the end of it.

Clown
O, he's drunk, Sir Toby, an hour agone; his eyes were set at eight i' the morning.

Oh, he's drunk, Sir Toby, for more than an hour now; his eyes where set at eight in the morning.
SIR TOBY BELCH

Then he's a rogue, and a passy measures panyn: I
hate a drunken rogue.

OLIVIA
Away with him! Who hath made this havoc with them?

SIR ANDREW
I'll help you, Sir Toby, because we'll be dressed together.

SIR TOBY BELCH
Will you help? an ass-head and a coxcomb and a knave, a thin-faced knave, a gull!

OLIVIA
Get him to bed, and let his hurt be look'd to.

SEBASTIAN
I am sorry, madam, I have hurt your kinsman:
But, had it been the brother of my blood,
I must have done no less with wit and safety.
You throw a strange regard upon me, and by that
I do perceive it hath offended you:
Pardon me, sweet one, even for the vows
We made each other but so late ago.

DUKE ORSINO
One face, one voice, one habit, and two persons,
A natural perspective, that is and is not!

SEBASTIAN
<u>Antonio, O my dear Antonio!
How have the hours rack'd and tortured me,
Since I have lost thee!</u> *and the boyfriends are reunited*

ANTONIO
Sebastian are you?

Then he's a rogue, and drunk: I hate a drunken scoundrel.

Away with him! Who has made all this confusion and commotion with them?

I'll help you, Sir Toby, because we'll be damaged together.

Will you help? [Flood of insults.]

Get him to bed, and let his hurt be looked after.

Exeunt Clown, FABIAN, SIR TOBY BELCH, and SIR ANDREW

Enter SEBASTIAN

*I am sorry, madam, I have hurt you relative:
But, had it been my own family,
I must have done just as much with cleverness and safety. You give me an odd look, and by that
I do see that it has offended you:
Pardon me, sweet one, even for the promises
We made each other just a few hours ago.*

One face, once voice, one set of clothes, and two people, A strange freak of nature!

*Oh Antonio, oh my dear Antonio!
How the hours have tortured me,
Since I lost you!*

Sebastian, is that you?

SEBASTIAN
Fear'st thou that, Antonio?

ANTONIO
How have you made division of yourself?
An apple, cleft in two, is not more twin
Than these two creatures. Which is Sebastian?

OLIVIA
Most wonderful!

SEBASTIAN
Do I stand there? I never had a brother;
Nor can there be that deity in my nature,
Of here and every where. I had a sister,
Whom the blind waves and surges have devour'd.
Of charity, what kin are you to me?
What countryman? what name? what parentage?

VIOLA
Of Messaline: Sebastian was my father;
Such a Sebastian was my brother too,
So went he suited to his watery tomb:
If spirits can assume both form and suit
You come to fright us.

SEBASTIAN
A spirit I am indeed;
But am in that dimension grossly clad
Which from the womb I did participate.
Were you a woman, as the rest goes even,
I should my tears let fall upon your cheek,
And say 'Thrice-welcome, drowned Viola!'

VIOLA
My father had a mole upon his brow.

SEBASTIAN
And so had mine.

VIOLA
And died that day when Viola from her birth
Had number'd thirteen years.

Are you afraid of that, Antonio?

*How have you made yourself two people?
An apple, cut in half, is not more twin
Than these two ones. Which is Sebastian?*

How strange!

*Do I stand there? I never had a brother;
Nor can there be magic in myself,
To be here and everywhere. I had a sister,
Whom the blind waves of the sea have devored.
Please, what relative are you to me?
What country, what name, what family?*

*Of Messaline: Sebastian was my father;
My brother was Sebastian too,
He went dressed like this to his watery grave;
If ghosts can take on both the form and clothing
You come to frighten us.*

*I am a spirit indeed:
But I am in this world, clothed in the body
Which I have had since the womb.
If you were a woman, as the rest is right,
I should let my tears fall upon your cheek,
And say, 'Three-times welcome, drowned Viola!'*

My father had a mole on his forehead.

So did mine.

*And when Viola was
thirteen years old.*

SEBASTIAN
O, that record is lively in my soul!
He finished indeed his mortal act
That day that made my sister thirteen years.

Oh, I remember that well!
He ended his mortal life
That day that made my sister thirteen years old.

VIOLA
If nothing lets to make us happy both
But this my masculine usurp'd attire,
Do not embrace me till each circumstance
Of place, time, fortune, do cohere and jump
That I am Viola: which to confirm,
I'll bring you to a captain in this town,
Where lie my maiden weeds; by whose gentle help
I was preserved to serve this noble count.
All the occurrence of my fortune since
Hath been between this lady and this lord.

If there is nothing else to make us happy
But this my male borrowed clothing
Do not embrace me till all the factors
Of place, time, fortune, do come together and jump That I am Viola: which to prove,
I'll bring you to a sea captain in this town,
Where lie my women's clothes; by whose gentle help
I was saved in order to serve this noble count.
Everything that has happened to me since
Has been between this lady and this lord.

SEBASTIAN
[To OLIVIA] So comes it, lady, you have been mistook:
But nature to her bias drew in that.
You would have been contracted to a maid;
Nor are you therein, by my life, deceived,
You are betroth'd both to a maid and man.

So that's it, lady, you have been mistaken:
But nature to her inclination made it right.
You would have been married to a girl;
Nor are you there, by my life, deceived,
You are engaged both to a man and a woman.

DUKE ORSINO
Be not amazed; right noble is his blood.
If this be so, as yet the glass seems true,
I shall have share in this most happy wreck.

Do not be distressed; his blood is noble.
If this is so, since it seems true,
I will have a part in this happy situation.

Boy, thou hast said to me a thousand times
Thou never shouldst love woman like to me.

To VIOLA
Boy, you have said to me a thousand times
That you should never love a woman the way you love me.

VIOLA
And all those sayings will I overswear;
And those swearings keep as true in soul
As doth that orbed continent the fire
That severs day from night.

And I will swear all those sayings again;
And keep them as true
as the sun.

DUKE ORSINO
Give me thy hand;
And let me see thee in thy woman's weeds.

Give me your hand;
And let me see you in your woman's clothes.

VIOLA

The captain that did bring me first on shore
Hath my maid's garments: he upon some action
Is now in durance, at Malvolio's suit,
A gentleman, and follower of my lady's.

OLIVIA
He shall enlarge him: fetch Malvolio hither:
And yet, alas, now I remember me,
They say, poor gentleman, he's much distract.

A most extracting frenzy of mine own
From my remembrance clearly banish'd his.
How does he, sirrah?

Clown
Truly, madam, he holds Belzebub at the staves's end as
well as a man in his case may do: has here writ a
letter to you; I should have given't you to-day
morning, but as a madman's epistles are no gospels,
so it skills not much when they are delivered.

OLIVIA
Open't, and read it.

Clown
Look then to be well edified when the fool delivers
the madman.

'By the Lord, madam,'--

OLIVIA
How now! art thou mad?

Clown
No, madam, I do but read madness: an your ladyship
will have it as it ought to be, you must allow Vox.

*Has my girl's dress: he is doing something
Right now for Malvolio,
A gentleman, and a servant of my lady's.*

*He shall explain thing: fetch Malvolio here:
And yet, oh dear, now I remember,
They say, poor gentleman, he's in a bad way.*

Re-enter Clown with a letter, and FABIAN

*A most terrible frenzy of my own
Made me forget about his.
How is he, sir?*

*He is doing as well as could be expected. Here
is a letter.*

Open it, and read it.

*Look then to be pleased when the fool saves
the insane man.*

*Reads
'By God, madam,'--*

What now! Are you insane?

*No, madam, I am only reading insanity: and if
your ladyship
will have it as it should be, you must allow it.*

OLIVIA
Prithee, read i' thy right wits.

Please, read in your right mind.

Clown
So I do, madonna; but to read his right wits is to read thus: therefore perpend, my princess, and give ear.

So I do, madam; but to read in his right mind is to read like this; therefore prepare yourself, my princess, and listen.

OLIVIA
Read it you, sirrah.

You read it, man.

To FABIAN

FABIAN
[Reads] 'By the Lord, madam, you wrong me, and the
world shall know it: though you have put me into
darkness and given your drunken cousin rule over
me, yet have I the benefit of my senses as well as
your ladyship. I have your own letter that induced
me to the semblance I put on; with the which I doubt
not but to do myself much right, or you much shame.
Think of me as you please. I leave my duty a little
unthought of and speak out of my injury.
THE MADLY-USED MALVOLIO.'

*I have been wronged and your drunken cousin has put me in darkness,
simply because I followed the instructions in the letter that you wrote,
and that I can show you. I have been treated terribly.*

OLIVIA
Did he write this?

Did he write this letter?

Clown
Ay, madam.

Yes, madam.

DUKE ORSINO
This savours not much of distraction.

This does not seem like insanity.

OLIVIA
See him deliver'd, Fabian; bring him hither.

She him rescued, Fabian; bring him here.

Exit FABIAN

To think me as well a sister as a wife,
One day shall crown the alliance on't, so please you,
Here at my house and at my proper cost.

DUKE ORSINO
Madam, I am most apt to embrace your offer.

Your master quits you; and for your service done him,
So much against the mettle of your sex,
So far beneath your soft and tender breeding,
And since you call'd me master for so long,
Here is my hand: you shall from this time be
Your master's mistress.

OLIVIA
A sister! you are she.

DUKE ORSINO
Is this the madman?

OLIVIA
Ay, my lord, this same.
How now, Malvolio!

MALVOLIO
Madam, you have done me wrong,
Notorious wrong.

OLIVIA
Have I, Malvolio? no.

MALVOLIO
Lady, you have. Pray you, peruse that letter.
You must not now deny it is your hand:
Write from it, if you can, in hand or phrase;
Or say 'tis not your seal, nor your invention:
You can say none of this: well, grant it then
And tell me, in the modesty of honour,
Why you have given me such clear lights of favour,

My lord if it may please you, these things further thought on, thought about,
To think as well of me as a sister as you would have a wife, One day shall celebrate the alliance, if it pleases you Here at my house and at my expense.

Madam, I am most pleased to accept your author.
To VIOLA
Your master releases you; and for your service done him,
So much against the inclinations of your sex,
So far beneath your station in life,
And since you called me Master for so long,
Here is my hand: you shall from now on be
Your master's wife.

Re-enter FABIAN, with MALVOLIO

Is this the insane man?

Yes, my lord, this is him.
How are you, Malvolio?

Madam, you have done me wrong,
A terrible wrong.

Have I, Malvolio? No.

Lady, you have. Please, read that letter.
You must not now deny it is your handwriting:
Write differently from it, if you can, in handwriting or style; Or say it is not your seal, or something you came up with: You can say none of this: well, going from there And tell me, honorably, Why you have made such indication of liking me,

Bade me come smiling and cross-garter'd to you,
To put on yellow stockings and to frown
Upon Sir Toby and the lighter people;
And, acting this in an obedient hope,
Why have you suffer'd me to be imprison'd,
Kept in a dark house, visited by the priest,
And made the most notorious geck and gull
That e'er invention play'd on? tell me why.

Telling me to come smiling and wearing crossed-garters to you,
To put on yellow socks and to frown
At Sir Toby and the less-important people;
And, doing as I was told, hoping for reward,
Why have you allowed me to be imprisoned,
Kept in a dark room, visited by the priest,
And been the victim of the worst prank
That anyone ever had to deal with? Tell me why.

OLIVIA
Alas, Malvolio, this is not my writing,
Though, I confess, much like the character
But out of question 'tis Maria's hand.
And now I do bethink me, it was she
First told me thou wast mad; then camest in smiling,
And in such forms which here were presupposed
Upon thee in the letter. Prithee, be content:
This practise hath most shrewdly pass'd upon thee;
But when we know the grounds and authors of it,
Thou shalt be both the plaintiff and the judge
Of thine own cause.

Unfortunately, Malvolio, this is not my handwriting, Though, I admit, very similar
But unquestionably it is Maria's handwriting.
And now it occurs to me, it was her
Who first told me you were insane; then came in smiling,
And in such a way that were hinted at
To you in the letter. Please, be calm:
This prank has very cleverly been done to you;
But when we know the reasons and culprits behind it,
You shall be both the plaintiff and the judge
Of your own case.

FABIAN
Good madam, hear me speak,
And let no quarrel nor no brawl to come
Taint the condition of this present hour,
Which I have wonder'd at. In hope it shall not,
Most freely I confess, myself and Toby
Set this device against Malvolio here,
Upon some stubborn and uncourteous parts
We had conceived against him: Maria writ
The letter at Sir Toby's great importance;
In recompense whereof he hath married her.
How with a sportful malice it was follow'd,
May rather pluck on laughter than revenge;
If that the injuries be justly weigh'd
That have on both sides pass'd.

Good lady, hear me speak,
And let no argument or fighting come
Ruin the happiness of this time,
Which has amazed me. Hoping it won't,
I freely confess that myself and Toby
Pulled this trick on Malvolio here,
Because of some stubbornness and rudeness
We had dealt with from him: Maria wrote
The letter for Sir Toby's sake;
In return for which he has married her.
It was all in good fun,
Please find it funny rather than worth revenge;
If it is considered fair the troubles
That both sides have endured.

OLIVIA
Alas, poor fool, how have they baffled thee!

Oh, poor fool, how they have outdone you!

Clown

Why, 'some are born great, some achieve greatness,
and some have greatness thrown upon them.' I was
one, sir, in this interlude; one Sir Topas, sir; but
that's all one. 'By the Lord, fool, I am not mad.'
But do you remember? 'Madam, why laugh you at such
a barren rascal? an you smile not, he's gagged:'
and thus the whirligig of time brings in his revenges.

MALVOLIO
I'll be revenged on the whole pack of you.

OLIVIA
He hath been most notoriously abused.

DUKE ORSINO
Pursue him and entreat him to a peace:
He hath not told us of the captain yet:
When that is known and golden time convents,
A solemn combination shall be made
Of our dear souls. Meantime, sweet sister,
We will not part from hence. Cesario, come;
For so you shall be, while you are a man;
But when in other habits you are seen,
Orsino's mistress and his fancy's queen.

Clown
[Sings]When that I was and a little tiny boy,
With hey, ho, the wind and the rain,
A foolish thing was but a toy,
For the rain it raineth every day.
But when I came to man's estate,
With hey, ho, & c.
'Gainst knaves and thieves men shut their gate,
For the rain, & c.
But when I came, alas! to wive,
With hey, ho, & c.
By swaggering could I never thrive,
For the rain, & c.
But when I came unto my beds,

*Why, 'some are born great, some reach greatness,
and some have greatness thrown upon them.' I was
a part, sir, of this business; one Sir Topas, sir;
but that's all the same. 'By the Lord, clown, I am not insane.' But do you remember? 'Madam, why do you laugh at such
an unfunny rascal? If you do not smile, he's gagged:' and in that way the wheel of time brings in his revenge.*

I'll have revenge on the whole bunch of you.

Exit

He has been most terribly treated.

*Follow after him and calm him down:
He has not told us about the captain yet:
When that is known and the time is right,
A serious union shall be made
Of our precious souls. Meanwhile, sweet sister,
We will not separate from here. Cesario, come;
For that is what you are, while you are a man;
But when in other clothes you are seen,
Orsino's wife and his love's queen.*

Exeunt all, except Clown

*When I was just a little tiny boy,
With a hey, ho, the wind and the rain,
A foolish thing was just a toy,
For the rain it rains every day.
But when I came to be a man
With hey, ho, etc.
Against villains and thieves men shut the gate,
For the rain, etc.
But when I came, oh no! To marry,
With hey, ho, etc.
By showing off I could never succeed,
For the rain, etc.
But when I came to my beds,*

With hey, ho, & c. With toss-pots still had drunken heads, For the rain, & c. A great while ago the world begun, With hey, ho, & c. But that's all one, our play is done, And we'll strive to please you every day.	*With hey, ho, etc.* *I was still drunk out of my mind,* *For the rain, etc.* *A great while ago the world began,* *With hey, ho, etc.* *But that's all the same, our play is done,* *And we'll try to please you every day.* *Exit*

Made in the USA
Coppell, TX
11 March 2020